DO IT YOURSELF HOME RENOVATION

SAVE MONEY, TIME, FRUSTRATION REMODELING YOUR HOME BY KNOWING WHAT TO DO, HOW TO BUY YOUR MATERIALS, AND WHEN TO CALL A PROFESSIONAL

BOB HOPKINS

ISBN : 978-1-63972-410-9

© **Copyright 2021 - All rights reserved.**

The content contained within this book may not be reproduced, duplicated or transmitted without direct written permission from the author or the publisher.

Under no circumstances will any blame or legal responsibility be held against the publisher, or author, for any damages, reparation, or monetary loss due to the information contained within this book, either directly or indirectly.

Legal Notice:

This book is copyright protected. It is only for personal use. You cannot amend, distribute, sell, use, quote or paraphrase any part, or the content within this book, without the consent of the author or publisher.

Disclaimer Notice:

Please note the information contained within this document is for educational and entertainment purposes only. All effort has been executed to present accurate, up to date, reliable, complete information. No warranties of any kind are declared or implied. Readers acknowledge that the author is not engaged in the rendering of legal, financial, medical or professional advice. The content within this book has been derived from various sources. Please consult a licensed professional before attempting any techniques outlined in this book.

By reading this document, the reader agrees that under no circumstances is the author responsible for any losses, direct or indirect, that are incurred as a result of the use of the information contained within this document, including, but not limited to, errors, omissions, or inaccuracies.

CONTENTS

Introduction ... 7

1. Getting to Know Your Home ... 13
2. Matters of Safety ... 33
3. Tools—Your Best Friends for Every Job ... 43
4. Power to Your Hands ... 61
5. Fasteners and Adhesives ... 87
6. Starting With Doors and Windows ... 111
7. The Sparks of Renovation—Electrical Projects ... 143
8. Renovating Your Home's Plumbing ... 167
9. Flooring It Right ... 185
10. Walls and Ceilings ... 203
11. A Definitive Guide to Wallpapers ... 215
12. The A-Z of Painting ... 227
13. HVAC Maintenance ... 241
14. Carpentry & Woodworking ... 251
15. Cabinets & Counters ... 263
16. Roof Repairs and Improvements ... 273
17. Exteriors and Backyard ... 285

Conclusion ... 297
References ... 301

Bob Hopkins

Do-It-Yourself

Home Renovation

RENOVATION IDEAS
Kitchen renovation · Bathroom renovation · Flooring · Plumbing · Painting · Heating and Air Conditioning · Solar · Electrical

Bob has a gift for you - his safety tips. Read the QR code or go to https://bob-hopkins.com/request-bobs-safety-tips.

SCAN ME

Never, never, never give up.

— WINSTON CHURCHILL

INTRODUCTION

As you reach your 20s and 30s, you undergo many life changes between establishing your career, managing your social life, and learning to manage your finances. Despite the chaotic situation, you may also be considering joining millions of young adults who bought or renovated their first home. Working professionals and young families have the buying power to own a home and invest in their living space as they become more financially independent.

Taking on the responsibility of owning a home for the first time and improving its aesthetic can be an exciting experience. Still, if you don't properly prepare, it can also be physically, mentally, and emotionally exhausting. No matter how old our homes are, nothing is guaranteed. Over time, even the properties we buy to feel secure and permanent fall into disrepair and need repair due to damage and wear. Every major home renovation and improvement agency is highly profitable in this sector.

If you are contemplating a renovation, you might be:

- Planning home renovations but ensuring you do the job right, but unsure how to follow through.
- Getting discouraged because you failed a DIY project.
- Thinking that you can see your project through to completion but are less confident than you appear to be.
- Weighing the pros and cons of hiring a professional simply because the costs are too high and saving money is your top priority.

Renovating your house requires a lot of research and planning. Wanting to minimize mistakes to get the most out of your limited time, you don't have time to perform a project multiple times. Your project may depend on completing it correctly the first time. Doing research is an essential step in planning. Make sure you research materials, labor costs, and contractors before deciding what you'd like to renovate. A third party can help manage your project by providing you with cost estimates for specific tasks or interviewing potential suppliers for electrical projects requiring a licensed contractor. Throughout the process, you'll be able to find out what is best when it comes to your project.

TAKE CHARGE OF YOUR MONEY

Renovations usually cost between $40K and $50K, but that's only true for a few projects. If you renovate your entire house, you could easily spend over $100K on the project. $100K is no small investment. You should avoid debt by paying renovation costs upfront if you have the cash on hand. Renovating isn't always budget-friendly, particularly if you're considering luxury features like above-ground pools. You should establish a budget accordingly and examine all financing options before you finalize your project plan.

Adding a buffer of about 10% to your budget is a brilliant idea because renovations rarely cost less than you initially expected. Then, in case an unforeseen expense occurs, you will be well-prepared. You will have a better renovation project if you approach it with a practical approach and a budget.

You may want to consider alternative financing options if you do not have enough money saved to pay for the project in full. For instance, you could apply for a credit card with low-interest rates or take out a personal loan. A home equity loan and renovations may be a good combination if you have enough equity in your home. In the case of newly purchased homes, even a few minor projects to make the property more usable can rack up a significant amount that could put a severe dent in the wallet.

I understand how intimidating it can be. The first time I owned a property, I wanted to make my home my own. My engineering skills, rather than being concerned about money, led me to take matters into my own hands and make simple repairs to improve and renovate my house slowly over several years. In my 20 years of home renovation and improvement experience, I can say that DIYing has allowed me to save a great deal of money and channel that money into things that matter.

I know what you're thinking. Even though DIY sounds good on paper, how do you create something that looks professional? In my journey, mistakes have been part of my learning curve, and I understand your hesitation.

The following are some things you will learn from this guide:

- Discover how you can carry out simple renovations and repairs on your own.
- You'll be able to save money and time when you do things on your own, and you will feel satisfied when you do something valuable and lasting.
- Knowing when to get professional assistance.

With clear, step-by-step instructions and various tips and techniques, you will not feel at a loss as you transform your work and boost your confidence.

ADAPTABILITY IS KEY

You may have an idea of what you want your renovation to look like, but factors such as weather, budgetary constraints, and time will all contribute to your ability to achieve it. Having an open mind is essential when doing any renovation project and preparing for when things don't go as planned.

My goal is to provide you with the proper knowledge of what to do and how to do it. Even if you don't have much money, you can give your home a facelift.

1

GETTING TO KNOW YOUR HOME

If this is your first time making home improvements, you may find it exciting and a little frightening at the same time. You need to prepare, put in the time, and budget well to accomplish your goals. Home renovations can range from minor cosmetic improvements to complete home remodeling. Whether you need to remodel your kitchen, install big beautiful windows, or even install solar panels, you have plenty of options to meet your needs.

THE DO-IT-YOURSELF ATTITUDE

You need to understand what you would like to achieve before you can begin renovating. If the vision is clear, it is easier to achieve it. Look through magazines, websites, architecture books, and other people's houses to create a mood board when you're stuck for inspiration.

You can start by assessing where you need to make improvements or where you wish to make more use of your space. Perhaps there are misaligned tiles or a failed sink in your kitchen, or your plumbing may leak constantly. A kitchen remodel in such a case might be necessary. A home improvement project goes much deeper than what you can see on the surface. Do you notice that cooling or heating is taking longer than it used to? If you are searching for one thing to work on in your home, grab a notepad and pen or take out your phone and tour each room with an eye on visual improvements, as well as picking out other home improvements that could improve your property.

Assuming your roof is in poor condition and looks shabby every time you pull into the driveway, do some research on various roofing types and decide what looks best with your home. You can make dealing with a contractor much easier if you have these ideas and examples in place. You will be able to visualize your home's potential and get a more accurate price estimate.

PLANNING

As part of your renovation plan, you need to clearly state your renovation goal, include inspiration for your designs, and outline the work to be done. Among the other items in your plan are:

- a blueprint or sketch of your finished project
- a list of the things that you will need to get the job done
- An outline of project steps categorized by what a DIYer can do versus what a professional can do.

Pick the desired start date and work backward from there, or if you want it done by a specific date, then work forward from the end date. Consult your contractor about the expected duration of each part of the project. It is best to discuss what remodeling steps are required first, how long they will take, and which components of the remodeling project can be completed simultaneously.

Ensure your timeline also includes

- cleaning up the project area is included
- deliveries of materials are included in this time as well
- remember to include holidays working on your project

Organize the steps of the project by using a calendar. Give yourself some wiggle room to deal with any unexpected issues after the completion date. Ensure the timeline is realistic and that you can stay within your budget.

Budget

Developing a budget and financing plan is the next step in planning a renovation. You should include the cost of permits, materials, cost of labor, and decorations. When your cost estimates do not fit your budget, you can eliminate project elements of lesser importance from your home improvement project plan.

Permits, Inspections, and Contractors

The proper building permits are essential when remodeling your home. You should take special care when working on this, even though it may seem confusing to most homeowners. Failure to do so would be very detrimental to your plans. It's your responsibility to get the permits if you plan to remodel your own home. You should first check if a permit is even needed for your project. In some cases, permits are required for even the most miniature work, while larger projects may qualify as repair work without permits.

Municipalities and counties issue building permits, which the local building department issues. Some renovations typically require a building permit in every municipality, including:

- the piping system has been modified
- electricity system changes
- HVAC system changes
- changes or additions in the house structure

- newly constructed windows or doors
- expansion beyond a set size of outbuildings
- overhanging decks
- changing the foundation of a building
- building a second apartment
- fireplace installation

Inspections are also required for a remodeling project. If the project is extensive, expect more than one inspection. A city may charge its residents 1% of the total remodeling cost as a fee for issuing the permit. Inspecting homes typically take around six weeks, so you need to be patient.

How Skipping the Permit Affects Your House

The authorities may shut down your project if they discover that it violates building codes. How the city responds to the infraction will depend on where you live. If you have in-progress construction, you may have to tear it down and start all over. In addition to doubling your construction costs, redoing your whole job will also exacerbate the stress.

Risk to Insurance Coverage

Your house insurance is invalid if you do not have a permit. Consider what would happen if a fire broke out or a collapsed wall injured someone. Your insurance company may not cover an unsafe construction site.

Complications With Your Property Sale

Public records exist for your building permit. A Property Disclosure Statement may be required by any future sellers of your house, stating whether your home has any problems. Loans for properties that do not have secured permits are generally not approved by lending banks. An individual using a loan to buy does not have the financial ability to close the deal. If you lack the proper paperwork, the entire process will become complicated. Doing this will either scare away potential buyers or decrease the property's resale value.

Working With Contractors

A licensed contractor must obtain permits from the building authority. They are experienced in applying for and obtaining permits. Remodeling a large part of your home may require the help of a team of professionals, including builders, electricians, plumbers, and more.

Typically, renovators need a contractor for

- construction of roofs and sideways
- plastering a drywall
- laying bricks
- building a waterproof foundation

Although you might handle these tasks safely in your own home if you know what you're doing, it is best to hire a professional to ensure the job is done correctly.

Utility Shut-offs

The following is a quick guide on locating and figuring out the utility electricity, water, and natural gas locations. To keep track of various things you discover and owner's manuals for your appliances, you might want to get a binder with plastic pocket pages.

As a result of the extra electricity used when renovating your house, you may notice an increase in your utility bills. During construction, you can expect to see your electric bill increase a few hundred dollars each month for each piece of equipment plugged in several hours per day or a small nail gun that is regularly used. Occasionally, the use of plumbing or electricity may require that utilities are turned off before you begin. By doing this, you will ensure there are no safety hazards present.

Water

In installing utility lines, a curb-stop is constructed underground to regulate the flow of water. Copper or plastic water lines are installed during home construction and provide water to the house. In case of an emergency or during renovations, you can close the curb-stop valve and interrupt the water supply to your home.

Sewer

Sewer pipes connect your home with the municipal sewer mains in your neighborhood. Gravity transports most wastewater from your sinks, showers, clothes washers, toilets, dishwashers, and other appliances to the sewer mains and onto the municipality's wastewater treatment plant.

Electricity

Utility companies lock up the pad-mount transformers connected to high voltage electrical lines since high voltages are dangerous. All electrical service that comes from the power plant into your home is under the control of the electric company. During the construction of your home, other electrical installations are handled by a licensed electrician.

Gas

Municipalities typically supply natural gas to residents through pressurized pipelines. The private gas lateral connected to the large gas main is also fitted with a valve, like a curb stop on a water line. It is easy to turn off the gas supply during a gas emergency or renovation if you do not need it.

Cable and Telephone

Traditionally, your phone line and cable TV line were installed by the telephone company. You would receive your phone service from the phone company, and you would receive a cable box from the cable company to connect to your television. It is incredible how quickly technology has changed in these areas and how quickly it continues. Most homeowners no longer use landlines as a result of smartphones' popularity. Computer use is continuously changing as a result of satellite and wireless technologies. Be sure to inquire about these services as you plan your home-building project to ensure that you build your home with today's most effective infrastructure.

Detectors and Alarms

Be sure you call the company you hired to install your alarm before starting. Planning can prevent almost every issue from occurring. It is also worthwhile to let the station monitor know if there are any anomalies when you are doing renovations.

Keep an Eye Out for Wires

Today's modern alarm systems are primarily wireless, but read your homeowner's manual thoroughly before commencing any disassembly. Check out a wire before cutting or damaging it if it looks unfamiliar to you or your contractors. You could end up paying a high price for the mistake.

Paint With Care

It is possible to paint some home appliances to coordinate with the decor, such as door sensors and motion detectors. Be sure to consult your security company before doing so. A motion sensor won't work if the infrared window is painted over. Having painted-over microphones makes a glass-break detector ineffective. A painted smoke detector or carbon monoxide detector may also cease to function.

Installing a New Door Sensor

You should be very cautious when getting a new door in an area where an alarm sensor once existed! Some sensors are wireless and can be moved to a new door relatively quickly; however, contractors have thrown out sensors along with the old door, so be aware of what and where they are. Changing the wires on wired sensors can be difficult in an old door frame, so you may want to contact your alarm company for assistance.

Watch Out for Power Lines

Alarm systems run almost exclusively on low DC power, so dealing with alarm wires is not too dangerous. However, connecting the wrong two wires can lead to severe damage to the equipment, requiring costly repairs.

Upon Completion, Run All Tests

Everyone wants to avoid discovering that a sensor on the front door wasn't hooked up properly three months after the renovation. When in doubt, do not hesitate to contact your alarm company. Open and close every door, walk in front of every motion, and make sure all the alarm zones register on your keypad. If you discover a problem before closing up your walls, it is easier to resolve.

Home Security

A home renovation or construction project may temporarily require you to relocate. Consequently, your belongings and home are left unsupervised each day when the construction crew goes. Motion sensors should monitor the construction of a new home during construction followed by a permanent burglar alarm after completion.

During any remodeling project, whether it be for your home or business, you should ensure that your burglar alarm, if applicable, is in functioning order during the project and especially after each day's construction work is completed. Motion-activated outdoor lighting, including temporary fencing around the property and a gate to allow you to enter and exit the property, is an essential security measure.

It might be beneficial to hire a security guard or install surveillance on a central site. A system for regularly inspecting the interior and perimeter of your home should be installed so that the guard can spot any leaks, smoke, or intruders. Your home should have cameras installed at the perimeter and throughout the interior.

Fire Prevention

A fire can spread throughout a home caused by an outdated electrical system or by using highly combustible building materials. An electrical fire began in another part of the house after a construction worker disabled the fire alarm system and left without realizing the property was in the final stages of construction. Despite the destruction of the home, they had insurance coverage in place to cover such losses. Following are some ways to ensure a fire does not damage you:

- On every level of your house and all over your worksite, keep enough fire extinguishers.
- If you plan to renovate your home, ensure that your fire alarm stays operational during construction.
- It is recommended to clean the workplace every day, including removing flammable materials and all rubbish.

Universal Design

Bathrooms

Bringing a bathroom up to date is an exciting project. It is vital to consider some less exciting concerns before deciding which new tile will suit your needs.

Choosing a bathroom look is the first step in remodeling. There are many factors to consider when selecting paint colors, tiles, vanities, showers, tubs, and faucets.. You can get overwhelmed very quickly, so do your research first. Starting with elements that you like, you can assemble a bathroom design that you like. You may decide the primary design element you want to incorporate into the bathroom design and then work your way around it. Considering who will use the bathroom, how it will be used, and how it will adapt to the rest of the house is all part of functional design.

The size of the bathroom, where the plumbing pipes and electrical wiring are located, and the typical dimensions of bathroom fixtures are just some of the natural factors that make a bathroom renovation critical. Thus, when you go to the store, ensure you have the specifications and measurements you need. Shopping without measuring is frustrating, but what is more frustrating is getting stuff that doesn't fit.

A renovation cannot be complete without remodeling or repairing fixtures and features, which could very well fit on their checklist: faucets, bathtubs, bidets, sinks, showers, toilets, and showerheads. Additionally, you should replace your mirrors and repair your shower doors. By changing out your door handles, drawer pulls, and shower door hardware, you can also change the look of your bathroom very quickly. You can completely transform your shower environment with new shower doors.

In wet rooms like bathrooms, ventilation is essential. Choosing the right fan, placing the installation correctly, and handling the electrical wiring are tricky tasks. You can get sick from damp, moldy bathrooms that lack proper ventilation. In addition to being a healthy bathroom, a well-ventilated room helps promote dental health. Air circulation can also prevent wood trim or fixtures from decaying and dry insulation from becoming saturated.

Kitchens

While remodeling your kitchen, most people do not know where to store their mail, and they are upset when they lose their bills because their routines are disrupted.

- Before you demolish your old kitchen, set up a temporary one.
- Ensure that any items, such as seasonings that need to be unpacked, are located in an easily accessible area.
- Make sure your boxes are marked. That will make unpacking much easier.
- You should relocate throw rugs located in the kitchen.
- You will need a secure place to store breakable objects such as framed photos, prints, and other wall-mounted collectibles. Vibrations generated by the tools may cause this material to fall off the wall or shelf and break.

The kitchen's gas, water, and electricity should be disconnected before the remodel begins. The plumbing pipes that connect the sink, dishwasher, and refrigerator should also be disconnected during remodeling to prevent flooding and leaking.

House Structure

Bearing vs. Non-Bearing walls

A wall that you intend to remove or to alter must be determined whether or not it is load-bearing or not. Removed portions of walls that bear loads must be replaced with adequate structural support, like beams or columns, which can support the same load as the removed portions.

A load-bearing wall supports the weight above it and is known as a retaining wall because of its ability to take a significant amount of weight. On the other hand, a partition wall is not a load-bearing wall; it only supports itself.

Load-bearing Exterior Walls

The exterior walls of a house surround its perimeter or the house's outer footprint. They are usually attached to the house's structure and bear some weight. Beams, or headers, span across tops of openings in the walls where windows and doors are present. A post is located on either side of each entrance to support the beam.

While this method does work, it would cost a lot more in terms of money. Typically, load-bearing exterior walls do not extend the entire length of a house. Although homes seem to have no external load-bearing walls, they usually have steel or wooden columns that connect the windows. The exterior view and the window glass take visual precedence, so the columns are almost invisible due to their size.

Joists

Load-bearing walls are generally not parallel to floor joists unless the wall in question is a beam. However, if the wall cuts perpendicular to the posts, it is likely to be load-bearing as well. It is possible, however, for a bearing wall to be parallel to the joists. Depending on the building design, it can be installed directly under each beam or on a block between two adjacent posts.

Roof Styles

Home roofs play a significant structural role. Despite its innocuous look, the roof's height implies that it poses a severe risk. On roofs, accidents are most common if a worker falls from a height, unsafe work surface, or bad weather.

Here are some of the most common safety hazards associated with roof repairs:

- stability of the roof
- security measures for ladders
- conditions outside
- rooster holes
- sensibility to the edges
- inadequate training
- fall protection equipment not used properly
- limited visibility
- ceilings with multiple levels and fall heights

Rather than performing DIY roof repairs, you should always hire a professional. You should never attempt roof repairs if you are not trained. To be safe working on the roof, the workers should wear safety harnesses, and weather conditions should be considered. Workers should use appropriate safety equipment, and you should always review the safety plan thoroughly.

The process of choosing a roof shape is more complicated than it appears. Roofs come in a wide variety of shapes and have distinct characteristics.

Gable Roof

When two roof pitches meet, they form a triangle. The roof is that spot where they merge. There are many advantages to a gable roof:

- They are easy to build.
- They shed water well.
- They're easily ventilated.
- They work with most house designs.

Hip Roof

Building a hip roof can be challenging because they usually have four sides. These roofs are popular, but they lack ventilation. These roofs are better suited to areas subject to high winds.

Dutch Roof

As the name suggests, a Dutch roof has hips and gable ends. By eliminating the lower part of the roof, access to the lower portion will be more accessible, and the top will have more natural light and space.

Mansard Roof

Several methods exist to construct this roof, but it is more complicated than hip and gable roofs. Each slope is divided into two parts. As the roof slopes downward, the pitch barely starts at the bottom. As a result, the inside of the house has more room, which usually leads to more space.

Flat Roof

It is essential to understand that most flat roofs are not entirely flat but low-sloped tops with a slope to allow runoff.

Shed Roof

It is often used as additions or with other roof styles. Shed roofs are similar to flat roofs, but they have a greater pitch.

Dormer Roof

Dormers are more like additions to existing roofs. They are an extension of the roof slope, which includes a window and a roof. Dormers add light and headroom to a room by utilizing the space created.

Renovation of your home can be a fun experience if you plan. If you are undertaking a home renovation project of any kind, prepare for possible issues first and then arrange to address them, as preparation is your best defense. The results you see when you complete a successful home improvement project will make the effort worthwhile.

2

MATTERS OF SAFETY

Before beginning any remodeling project, take the time to plan and prepare appropriately. It would help if you had all of the safety equipment necessary for the task you will perform to protect your health and the health and safety of your family. By using personal protective equipment (PPE) when remodeling, you reduce your exposure to toxins.

TOXINS TO BE AWARE OF

Asbestos

Before 1990, dwellings were constructed using asbestos, a fibrous substance. Asbestos was considered an excellent construction material because of its strength, durability, and fire resistance. Then it was found that exposure to it might lead to deadly illnesses like mesothelioma. Only professionals should handle asbestos. Consider hiring a qualified asbestos assessor or remediator when planning your remodeling. They can inform you whether your home has asbestos and advise how to treat it or have it removed.

Lead-Based Paint

Lead-based paint was most likely used on your house if it was constructed before 1970. Before sanding or repainting, do a lead-based paint test on any painted surfaces. Lead is a poisonous metal that accumulates in the body to lethal quantities if exposed repeatedly. Due to sanding and grinding, there may be significant lead contamination in the air or food while working with lead-based paints. Infants, expectant mothers, and unborn children are especially vulnerable.

Mold

Mold may grow in bathrooms, laundry rooms, kitchens, and beneath moist or poorly aired carpets. A mold retardant may be added to paint when painting walls or other moisture-sensitive surfaces. When mold spores are discharged and breathed in, they may cause allergic responses and respiratory difficulties, so it's critical to remove mold properly and plan for future mold growth prevention while you rebuild.

PUT ON PROPER PROTECTIVE GEAR

We have all undertaken a home improvement project at some point in our lives. Consider your last project. Whether you constructed the mosaic end table you've always wanted, or you did it out of a need to repair a leaking faucet, chances are you might have benefitted from some safety gear. No matter how inexperienced you are at in-home repairs and construction, you should have a few critical items of safety equipment on hand just in case. If you use these five essentials, your renovation will be safer and more enjoyable!

Protective Eyewear

Safety goggles shield your eyes from flying debris such as dust, wood chips, and metal shavings while you're working with power equipment. Toxic solvents such as furniture varnish, polish, and ordinary home cleansers are also protected by eye protection. You can get them at a low price, and they're readily accessible. Before you buy any, make sure that they are the right size for your face and that you try them on first.

Earplugs

Loud tools like a jackhammer, chainsaw, or drill are required for specific home improvement work. Insert earplugs to protect your eardrums before you begin these chores. Your eardrums are more sensitive than you may realize. If you use a lawnmower, leaf blower, or woodworking equipment for long periods, you're putting yourself at risk for hearing loss due to noise-induced damage. Even more regrettable is the fact that the damage to your inner ear is irreversible. There are over-the-counter and bespoke canal plug options.

Gloves

A nice pair of all-purpose work gloves is a must-have for household chores. To make your life easier, choose a set of gloves that are well-suited to the jobs you do regularly. Snug-fitting designs allow you to feel what you're doing through the fabric, making handling objects more straightforward. When working with heavy or sharp things that have the potential to penetrate your flesh, such as furniture or planks made of wood that might splinter, make sure you wear gloves. When dealing with little things, gloves with gripping material on the inside of the hand or the fingers might come in handy.

Clothing That Offers Protection

Do-it-yourself tasks dictate what supplies you need on hand. It's critical to stock your DIY toolkit with safety attire. An oversized T-shirt or apron may be all you need around the house to protect your skin and clothes from cleaning chemicals like bleach. Inexpensive disposable coveralls provide full-body protection from things like dust and chemicals.

Wear sturdy work boots that protect your feet from all sides while working with heavy equipment, such as if you drop something on them or tread on a sharp item. If you often use risky equipment like a lawnmower or weed wacker, have a pair of steel-toe boots on hand.

Cover your exposed skin while dealing with chemicals to avoid skin burns, contamination, or allergic reactions. Use masks to prevent breathing toxic substances while painting, working with chemicals, removing asbestos, or just being around dust.

Protect Work Zones With Warning Tape

Use a medium-tack tape for the majority of your projects. "Safe Release" and "Clean Release" are examples of cassettes with these designations. As an alternative, there are high-adhesion tapes for tough to conceal surfaces like brick and low-adhesion tapes for delicate wallpapers. The best assortment of tape may frequently be found at a paint shop.

As soon as the tape is removed, do all you can to avoid damage. Over time, the adhesive reinforces the connection. Masking tapes have a shelf life ranging from one to fourteen days, depending on the glue used. Please pay attention to the label and follow the instructions on it.

Even an expensive countertop becomes a workstation or storage shelf when placed in a work area. Covering counters with cardboard will help to keep them scratch-free. You should use clean cardboard and wipe the surface off before the cardboard is laid down. To prevent the garbage from entering and cardboard from sliding about, tape the edges. Use cardboard strips to cover the outer edges as protection. Alternatively, you may purchase manufactured protective corners online or just cut them out of solid shipping boxes. When removed, the painter's tape will not harm the paint, so make sure the cardboard reaches at least four feet above the surface you're painting.

Protect your floors with a pair of shoe coverings instead of trailing dirt all over the place. To go into a room without floor protection, you don't have to take off your shoes or boots and replace them. Booties are inexpensive and may be found at home improvement stores.

WORKING UP HIGH

Even if just a few feet above the ground, working at heights should always be done with extreme caution. If you're in the hospital because you fell off a ladder or slipped off the roof, a beautiful paint job or a brand new kitchen will mean nothing to you. Use a 75-degree angle to set the base of a straight or extension ladder. Make sure your body is centered between the ladder's rails and avoid attempting to move the ladder while on it.

Do not put a ladder in front of an unlocked or partially obstructed door. Do not allow anything that might cause a sliding hazard, such as oil, grease, or paint on the ladder rungs or other surfaces. Remove any tools, hoses, cables, or other debris from the area where you will place the ladder. Never move an extension ladder while it is extended; always collapse the ladder before moving it even a short distance. Please make sure the extension ladder's locks are in place before attempting to use it.

Use a Ladder Stabilizer to Help You Climb

Use an adjustable ladder stabilizer while working on the windows or roof of your upper level. These devices, often constructed of aluminum, connect to the top of a ladder and provide the ladder with four contact points, increasing its stability. Stabilizers assist in avoiding ladder movement and sliding by distributing the weight across a greater surface area. Using a stabilizer also makes working on things like windows right in front of the ladder easier.

ITEMS TO BE COVERED

Blinds and Drapes That Wrap Around the Windows

All dust-gathering apertures in windows should be sealed with plastic. Cover the window coverings with plastic instead of taking them off while opening windows. You should approach removing window coverings with caution: Metal slats bend, cloth tears, and parts vanish. Repairing damaged treatments may be costly, and finding a replacement that matches can be difficult. Using masking tape attach plastic to the casing's top, and then tuck it beneath and behind the container itself.

The plastic backing of the window treatment should be taped to the window's top jamb once it has been opened. Remove the screens before you begin. The use of screens during building is a no-no. Removing any screens from windows and doors that might be in danger is a necessary first step in any renovation project. Make sure to label each one so that they can all be traced back to their original location. Please place them in a secure, out-of-the-way spot after wrapping them in plastic.

Cover the Vents

Return air ducts may get clogged with construction dust. It's much worse when microscopic dust particles get past the filter and wind up in every room in the home, creating a fine dust cloud. When your heating/cooling system kicks on, dust that has settled within the supply ducts will be sucked right out. The damper on a supply register may be closed, but it will not be as good at sealing out dust as plastic and tape. While the ducts are covered, make sure the heating/cooling system is turned off. Using the system at a low airflow setting might cause harm to the components.

FIRST-AID KIT

When working on home improvement tasks, there's always the risk of being hurt. A basic understanding of first aid will serve you well. Make sure you know a little about first aid if you're working on a dangerous job. Apply pressure on the wound if the victim is bleeding. Always clean and cover cuts and scratches throughout the day. If they've been stabbed, don't try to remove the weapon; instead, contact an ambulance right away.

3

TOOLS—YOUR BEST FRIENDS FOR EVERY JOB

The initial cost in assembling a well-built home-improvement toolbox is usually modest. As you improve in specific areas, you'll be ready to level up and purchase new tools that will allow you to work on more varied tasks in the future.

MASTERING THE TOOLS

Screwdrivers

Screwdrivers are useful household items to have on hand. They're wonderful for home improvement projects, but you'll also need them for smaller repairs and maintenance jobs around the house, like changing batteries in toys or tightening up some loose hardware. As a result, a set of screwdrivers that can drive the most common screws is highly suggested.

Pliers

With pliers, you can cut wiring, replace showerheads, fix bent plugs, or stabilize objects with your hands. Some of the most common pliers are simple slip-joint pliers, channel lock (brand name) pliers, and electrical pliers which are shown following.

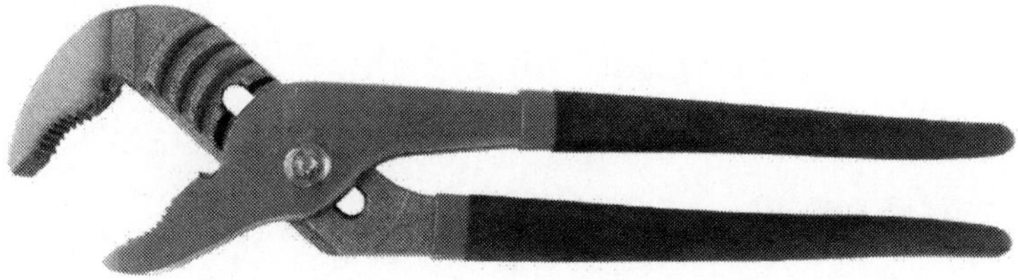

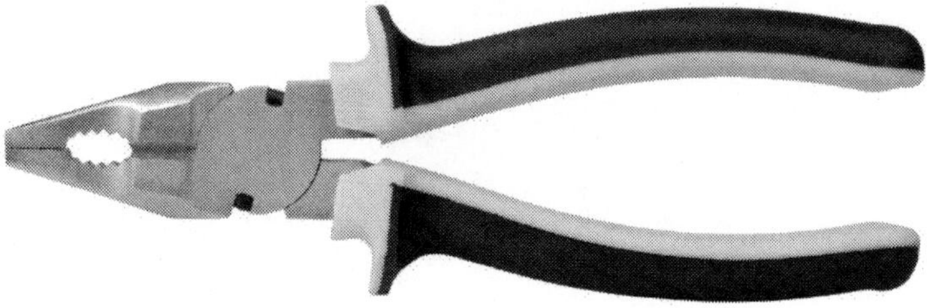

Square Speed

You might think the speed square is the most dangerous tool if you're new to do-it-yourself renovations. A small number of users remark that using it is like trigonometry, whereas most find it simple. It allows you to accurately cut and hole dimensional timber by taking measurements and marking lines on it.

Adjustable Wrench

Many household appliances, playground equipment, and even plumbing fixtures require wrenches throughout the assembly and tightening process. There are two standard sizes: a 6-inch and a 10-inch handle. It's best to use the shorter one while working in confined locations, while the longer one is ideal for when you need more leverage to loosen a stubborn nut. An 8-inch size is shown.

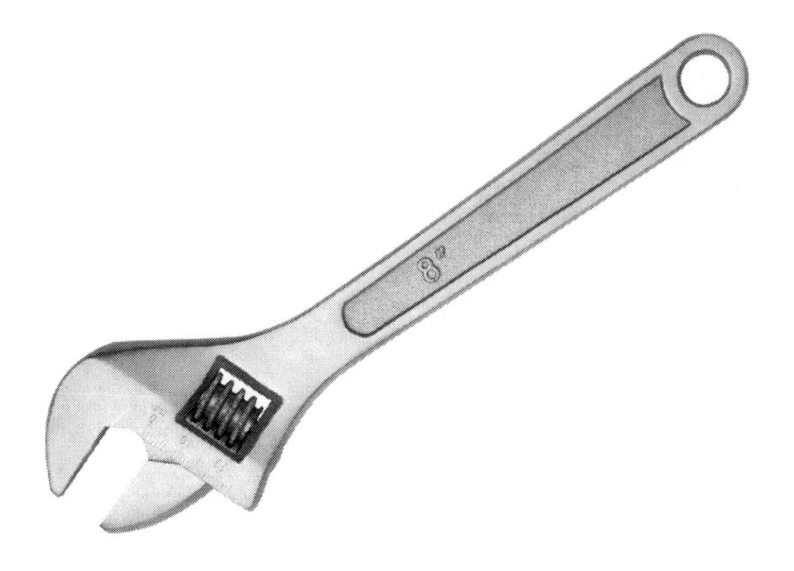

Hammer

Drive nails using a hammer with a curved claw for basic projects such as ready-to-assemble furniture sets, birdhouses, or pictures hanging on the wall. If you're disassembling something and need to remove the nails from adjoined pieces, the curved claw comes in handy.

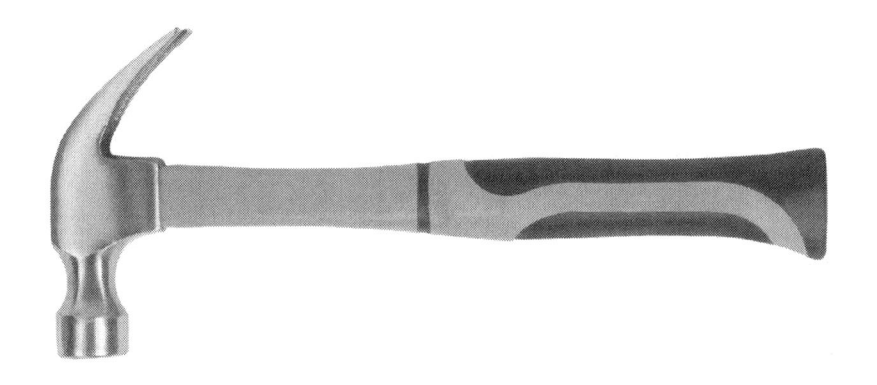

Putty Knife

Scraping, spreading, or re-glazing are standard methods of using a putty knife. It can assist you in cleaning any surface or in applying things uniformly.

Measuring Tape

It doesn't matter what kind of renovation project you're working on at home; you'll eventually get into a situation where you need to take measurements. Numbers, as you'll see, are critical when it comes to delivering high-quality work.

Hand saw

A sharp hand saw can teach you the fundamentals of molding stock and wood trimming before investing in a power saw. Using this method, you'll improve your accuracy when measuring and cutting.

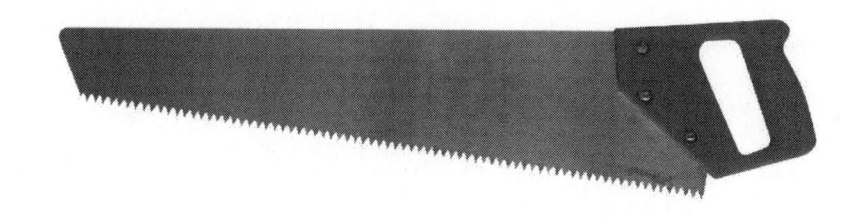

Chisels

When you have the wood for your project nearly the way you want it, you will need to make some fine adjustments to it. Door jambs, and the recesses and openings for the door hardware, will need to be adjusted just a bit. Cabinet work may not fit quite the way you want. You will need some chisels to remove small portions of wood before the job is complete. The picture also shows some wood rasps and wood files. Those will come in handy if you take your cabinet or other woodworking to the next level.

Level

A level will tell you when your chosen frame of reference is horizontal concerning the earth's surface. Each vial of liquid contains an air bubble, and when the air bubble is squarely in the center, you are level.

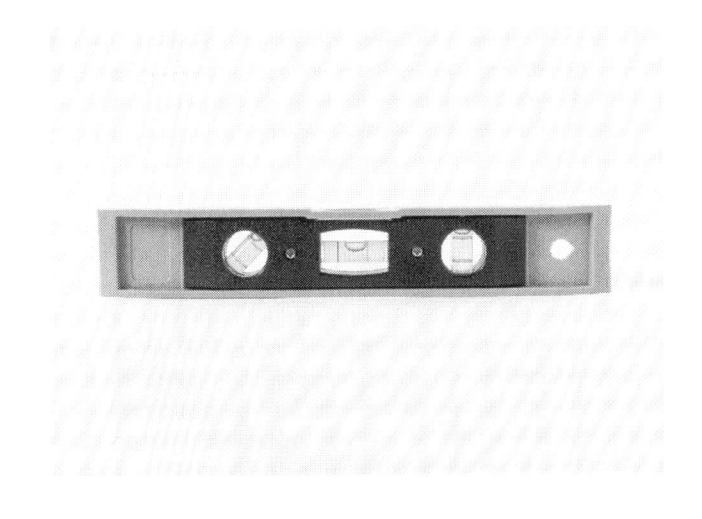

Duct Tape

Duct tapes are commonly seen in emergency kits for a reason. The reason for this is that they're good enough to serve as a temporary remedy when anything is ripped or broken.

Ladders

Ladders are available in a variety of styles. Step stools, step ladders, and A-frame ladders are frequently utilized in house renovation work. When you only need a few more feet of height to complete the task at hand, these solutions are perfect.

Set of Sockets

Socket sets make it easier to put together things that use nuts and bolts. Socket sets, rather than manually tightening everything, reduce the likelihood of bolts being dangerously loose. If you do a comprehensive makeover, home renovation projects may also require demolition work.

Sledgehammer

When smashing concrete, sledgehammers utilize the user's momentum and long handle, and oversized head. In most cases, this is used in rehabilitation projects that necessitate the removal of existing walls.

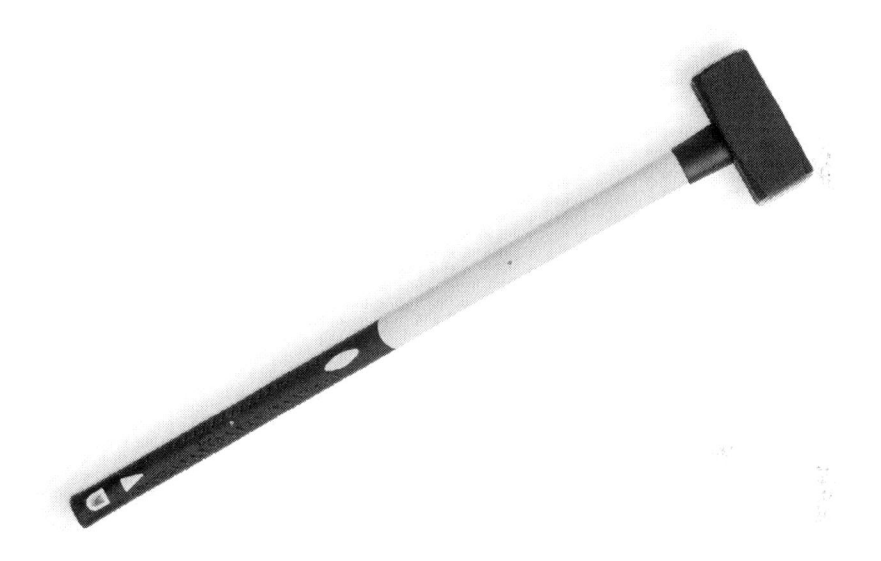

Crowbar

Crowbars are used to open nailed containers or to rip apart timber boards. You can also use them to unstick two things that were previously attached.

Paint Brushes

If you're going to be painting a lot, these are great tools in which to invest. You should use a small angled brush to paint small details such as window frames and sills, which will allow you to reach every small nook and cranny. Additionally, natural bristle paint brushes usually require a little bit of time to break in, so synthetic brushes are usually better if you only need them for one project or if you have an infrequent need for small ones.

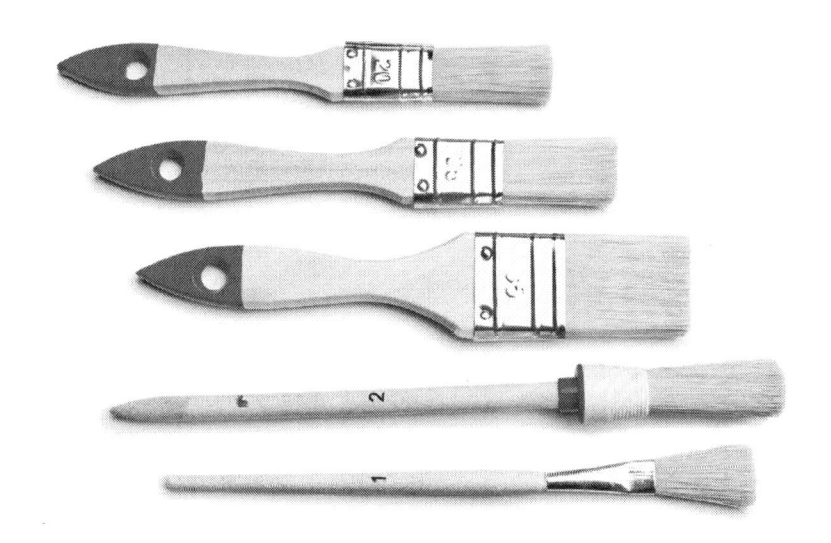

YOUR TOOLBOX SHOULD REFLECT YOUR CURRENT LEVEL OF EXPERTISE

If you're a do-it-yourselfer, your objectives are probably a reflection of your ability level. Most likely, as you gain experience and get better at managing more challenging jobs, you'll want to move up in the project hierarchy. While it may be alluring to get the most cutting-edge gear you come across, you should first determine if your talents and projects necessitate it. Advanced tools only have their full potential when held by a skilled user. For the time being, it's best to limit your purchases to the necessities, such as construction tools you'll use regularly. As your skills in house remodeling and renovation develop, you'll be better able to determine which tools will improve the appearance of your work.

4

POWER TO YOUR HANDS

People who use power tools at home seem to cope better with crises. If you attempt to fix anything on your own, only having hand tools at home may not be sufficient. Power tools are also necessary since they enable you to repair or build anything at any time. Furthermore, power tools are more efficient and user-friendly than manual tools. A jigsaw, miter saw, reciprocating saw, cordless drill, paint sprayer, hammer drill, wood router, and random orbital sander are among the tools available. Here's why every home should have these power tools.

SIMPLE REPAIRS

How many times have you hired a contractor to solve a small problem in your home? If you often call a professional to repair a broken door or a loose cabinet, you should invest in power equipment. These tools will save you money in the long term since you will no longer need to call a contractor every time anything breaks; instead, you will be able to repair it yourself.

LEARN HOW TO DO IT YOURSELF

Having power tools at home allows you to experiment with new activities. When you have power tools at your disposal, you will discover an infinite number of things you can develop or design to make your daily life simpler. You may read a power tools blog to learn how to utilize the tools and what you can accomplish with them. For example, if you want to create wooden products, you may master the fundamentals of woodworking and enhance your talents.

CONSTRUCTION

When you have your power tools, you may readily build a modest shed in your garden or a shelter for your pet. Doing it yourself will save you a lot of money since you won't need to employ a professional to do it for you; instead, you'll need to buy the tools you'll need for the construction you want to create.

RENOVATING

You can accomplish certain things yourself if you have the right tools. With the correct power tools and a few additional pieces of equipment, you can efficiently complete kitchen upgrades, floor installation, and door replacements. However, to effectively remodel your home, you must understand utilizing this equipment and know which materials to employ.

MUST-HAVE POWER TOOLS FOR YOUR DIY PROJECTS

Many of these items need adequate safety and precautions and are more of a professional's manner of doing things. As a result, people should consider these tools only if they need them or want to practice and work on them regularly to gain confidence. Otherwise, many DIY hardware and home improvement stores provide cutting services in some form, and novices may use them to obtain the necessary cuts.

ADVANTAGES OF POWER TOOLS

To be prepared for any emergency, every home should have a few essential power tools. You can fix many things around your home with the right tools. However, if you lack power tools or don't know how to use them, you'll have to pay a contractor every time anything has to be fixed, which is a waste of money. When you have the power tools you need, keep them adequately maintained to minimize damage and increase their lifespan. Power tools should be kept in a dry, out-of-the-way location where they may be quickly accessed as needed. To protect your safety, you should take the time to learn how to utilize these tools.

Circular Saw

When the miter saw and Jigsaw fail to reach the needed cutting length or precision of the cut, this tool will come in handy. The circular saw will give you an even cut along the side of a piece of wood. They are available in corded or cordless versions, as well as a variety of other configurations. They may save a significant amount of time on sheet material cuts, making them an essential need for any house repair.

Miter Saw

You'll need to buy a miter saw if you don't already have one. These robust tools can cut at a range of various angles. They feature a circular blade that revolves at high speed. The blade is linked to an arm, which you draw down to cut your workpiece, placed on a table underneath the blade. They're simple and basic to operate, making them an excellent alternative for novices. You can use a miter saw to cut a variety of materials. They are, however, ideally suited for crown molding, door frames, and other applications that need precise angle cuts.

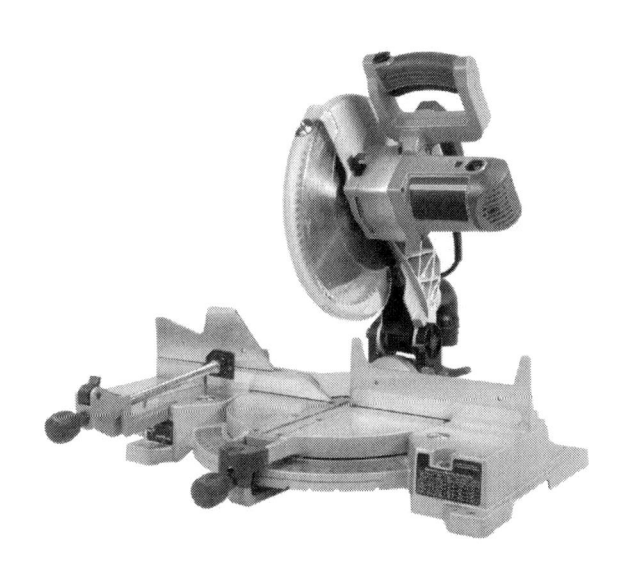

Reciprocating Saw

In terms of demolition equipment, reciprocating saws are unbeatable due to their ability to cut through practically everything except concrete. If you use the corded version, you'll need an extension cable to run your tool if the power outlet is too far away.

Jigsaw

A jigsaw is a powerful tool that makes it simple to generate curved cuts on items such as sheets of wood. Jigsaws are unquestionably the most affordable and user-friendly power equipment available. They are available at a variety of costs, although none are too expensive. Avoid the cheapest and strive for something in the mid-range to guarantee a good tool that will allow some accurate cuts. You may also buy several cordless ones from the same manufacturer with interchangeable batteries.

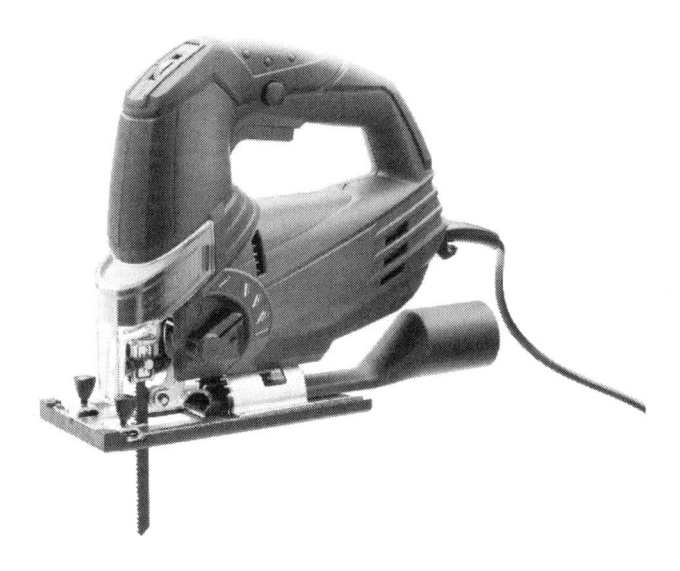

Chainsaw

Most people understand what a chainsaw is and should have one in their workshop just in case. They may be powered by batteries or gasoline. However, gasoline is still the most common choice nowadays. These gadgets need a lot of upkeep and might be harmful. However, when handled correctly, they are no more hazardous than the majority of the other power tools on this list. This tool is exceptionally versatile since it can cut a wide range of materials. While most chainsaws are only built for wood, some are specifically designed for concrete and stone.

Cordless Drill

Drivers and Drills

If you're going to buy a power tool, you should get a cordless drill. These drills are often powered by a battery, making them very portable. They are also strong enough to drive screws into thicker materials, such as wood boards. They're utilized for a variety of tasks. If you need to drill a hole in a wall, wood, or other challenging surfaces, this equipment may help. There are corded choices as well, but they are not as portable as their cordless counterparts.

When using a cordless drill, you can make holes in wood and screw things in place with ease. It's commonly used in woodworking and furniture assembly. Models with more horsepower are more suitable for renovating if you must use them that way.

Impact Driver

Although an impact driver and a cordless drill may be used for similar purposes, several fundamental differences distinguish these two pieces of equipment. An impact driver resembles a cordless drill, but it employs a pounding movement and raw power to do tasks. The impact driver and the cordless drill are excellent for minor operations since they provide superior control while operating at various speeds and clutch settings. Your impact driver drives screws with extraordinary power by using concussive blows and a little rotating. It features a keyless chuck and can take a variety of attachments. It delivers continuous torque and has a broad range of functions.

Drill Bits

The sort of drill bit you choose is determined by the material you want to drill. Drill bits are classified into three types:

Drill Bits for Metal

Metals may be drilled using metal drill bits that have a partly ground tip. Aluminum, copper, brass, zinc, iron, and non-alloy steel are among them. For stainless steel, drills manufactured of cobalt-alloy High-Speed Steel or drill bits with a titanium coating are required. These are more costly than standard HSS drill bits, but they allow for drilling in specific steel without causing excessive drill bit wear.

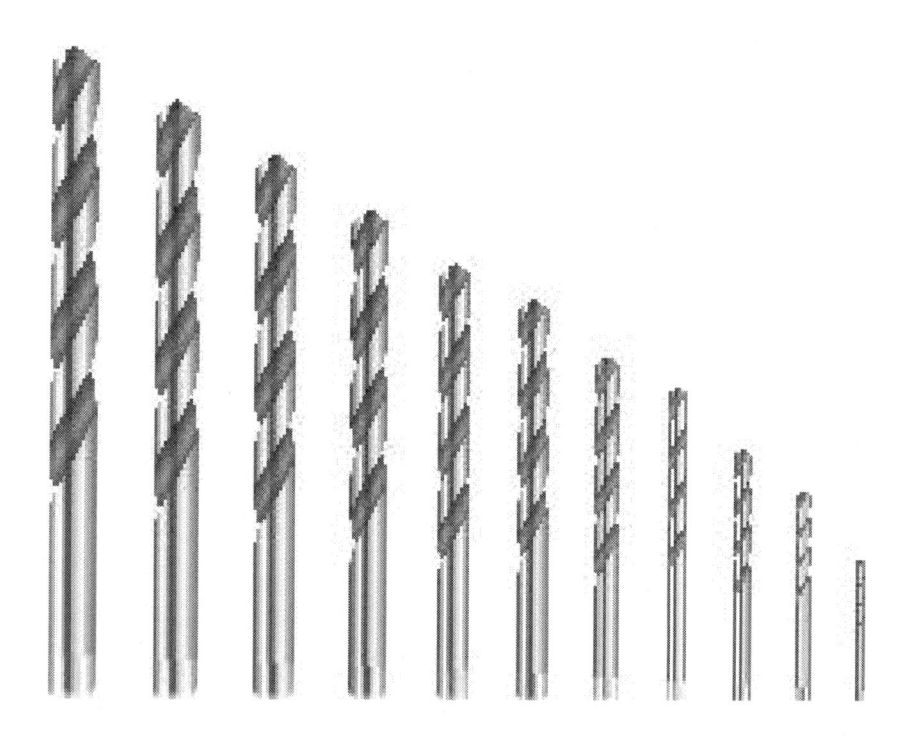

Drill Bits for Wood

These contain a long centering tip and two pre-cutting spurs, making them ideal for drilling neatly into the wood.

SDS Drill

An SDS Drill—also called a Rotary Hammer, is used to drill holes in fully cured concrete. It speeds up making a hole in concrete—either for a concrete anchor or to put something through a concrete slab.

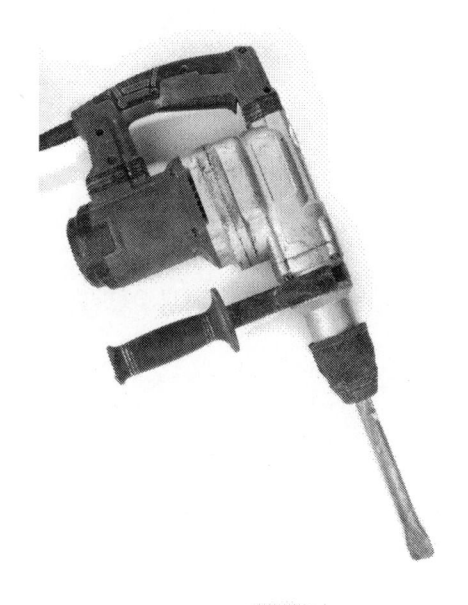

Drill Bits for Concrete

These are used in conjunction with a hammer drill or an SDS drill to drill into masonry and concrete (an SDS drill is required for drilling in concrete). However, only rotational drilling is used if the wall is composed of porous perforated stones. The same is true for permeable brickwork and boarded-up walls. Use a masonry drill bit with soldered-in tungsten-carbide plates on the drill tip for drilling in these materials.

Angle Grinder

Cutting pavers and tiles is easy with a high-quality angle grinder. In addition to sharpening, polishing, and sanding surfaces, it can also grind metal and rout out masonry.

Simply changing the grinder's wheel will do the trick, depending on what you need to do. As a result, the angle grinder is an excellent choice if you're seeking a versatile power tool. An electric motor, pressurized air, or a gasoline engine may power the angle grinder. The angle grinder's motor powers a right-angled gearhead with an abrasive disc or a little cut-off disc, both of which may be changed as they wear out. Depending on how quickly they run, certain angle grinders may also be used as sanders by connecting a sanding disc and a disc or backing pad. Depending on your product's flexibility, a support system often comprises hard plastic, medium-hard rubber, or phenolic resin.

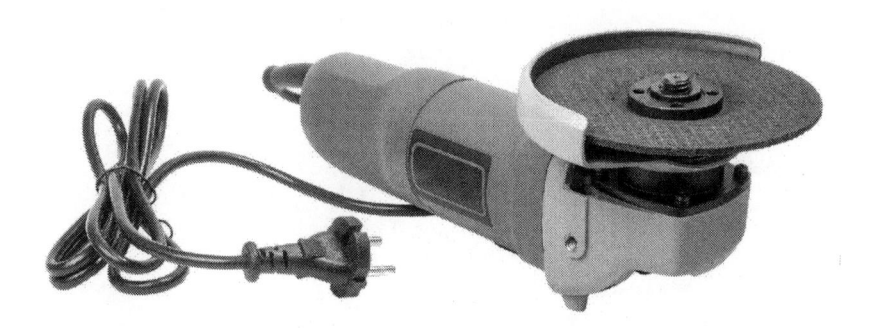

Sanders

A sander will be required for the majority of do-it-yourself jobs. Even if you try to avoid it, you will use a sander at some point in your DIY project if it is of high quality. An electric sander is the most basic type of sander. You can use them to smooth the surface of the wood after sanding it. Belt sanders come in handy when working on larger projects that require a flawless finish. When it comes to smoothing flat surfaces and edges, an orbital finishing sander is an excellent tool for beginners because it's lightweight and easy to use.

Sander With an Orbital Motion

You will almost always need to utilize an electric sander during a home repair project. The general contractor, as well as the do-it-yourselfer, should have this tool. If you're going to do something substantial, prepare to be patient, tired, and possibly dissatisfied. Using an electric sander will save you time and make your project seem better in the end.

Palm Sander

This power tool, often known as an elbow sander, can sand practically any surface. It also saves time and effort. You may avoid the agony of painful elbows and wrist strain by utilizing a palm sander. It is advisable to use a cordless palm sander for optimal ease. The battery component, on the other hand, adds weight and girth to the gadget. The battery may make it tough to navigate. Fortunately, the corded version is lighter. Even though you must plug it into a power outlet, it is less laborious and more versatile to operate. It would help if you connected sandpaper to the sander. As a result, make sure you have some additional sandpaper on hand for any home improvement work.

Oscillating Tool

An oscillating tool is another helpful power tool that you may use for a wide range of activities. Woods and floors can be trimmed, metal rusts removed, masonry and old paint removed, apertures in walls cut, and furniture sanded with this tool.

Air Compressor With a Nail Gun

When it comes to significant operations like framing, roofing, and trim work, nothing beats the convenience of a nail gun and air compressor. Finish work necessitates using a nail gun because banging nails by hand usually result in a shoddy job. Nail guns are available in various gauges, and they can all be used with the same compressor and air hose.

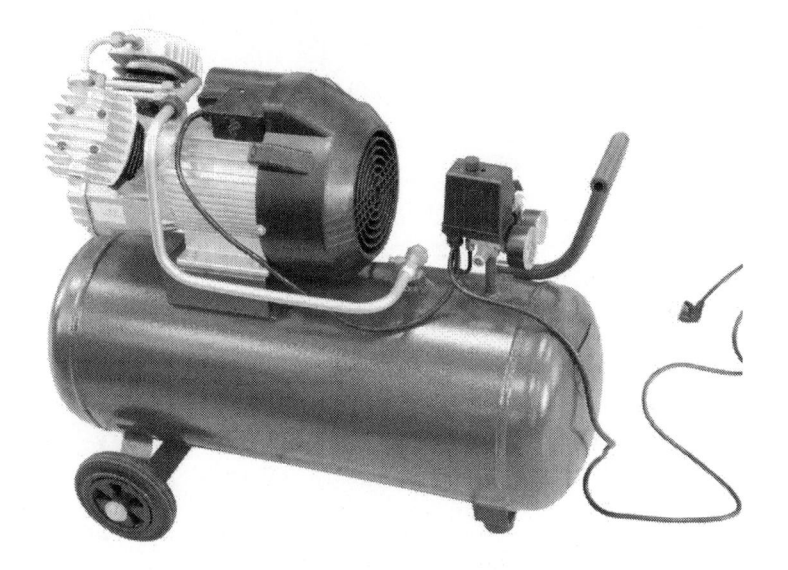

Air Hose

Most compressors and air tools will come with no hose. You will need at least one air hose and a set of accessories. Among those accessories will be several fittings for the end of the hose. Make sure you have one for the compressor end and one for each tool you buy.

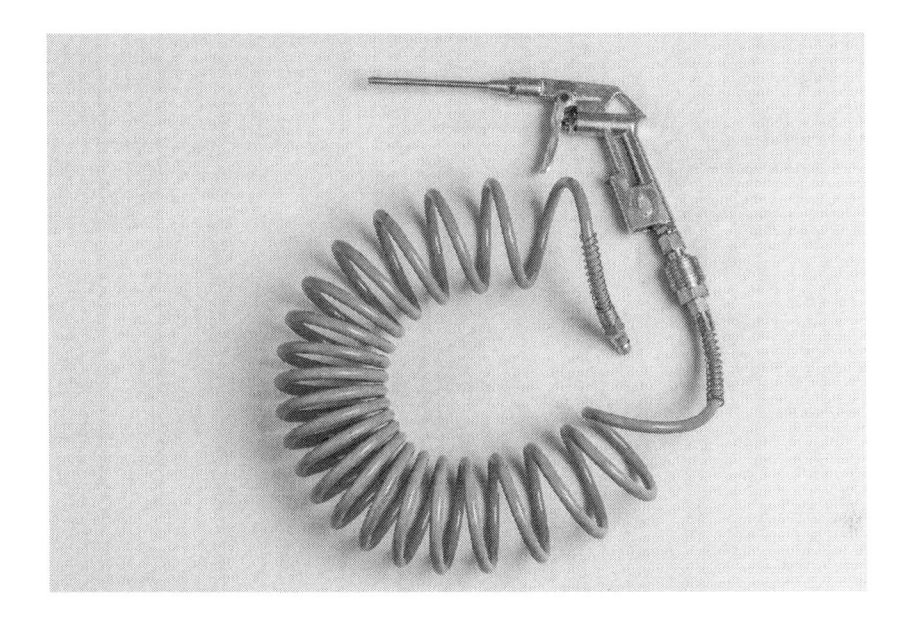

Nailer

A nailer, as the name implies, is a powerful tool for driving nails into various materials. When used with hammers, Nailers will take your home improvement skills to the next level because of their accuracy and speed. Nail guns are a type of power tool that fires nails. It's as simple as that. They serve as a replacement for hammers and are helpful for any project that requires nails. If you're going to be using a lot of nails, a nail gun could come in handy. The majority of them are powered by compressed air, but electric models are also available. There are several nail guns available, depending on the size of the nail you need to use.

Air Impact Wrench

An impact wrench is a kind of wrench that applies a lot of force with minimal effort from the operator. They generate a tremendous amount of torque. Typically, pressurized air is utilized, although electric variants are now available. These are excellent for releasing overly tight lug nuts or removing stripped screws. You should keep at least one of these in your toolbox since you never know when you'll need to remove a seemingly impossible-to-release lug nut. You will need another set of Air Impact sockets for it in addition to your smaller socket set.

Paint Sprayer

Some prefer to paint with a brush or roller, but this requires a significant amount of time and work. A power paint sprayer will enable you to paint a wall quickly. You will also be able to paint uneven surfaces with ease.

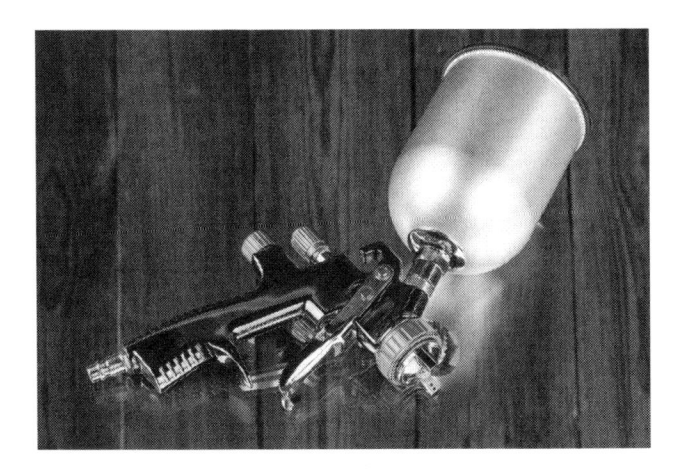

Shop Vacuums

The shop vac is a kind of vacuum that is often used in woodworking and building. The shop vac is a powerful motor unit with great suction that can take up a lot of construction materials, garbage, and dirt. These vacuums include a long, durable hose and an extra-large canister to retain the trash they collect. They are well-known for their ability to clean even the dirtiest of environments. One of its characteristics is the wheels on which they sit, which allow them to move about in any location. These are the not kind of vacuums you'd use to clean your home since they're designed for huge chores.

Generator for Emergency Power

Though this won't be part of your toolbox, you will need it when working on your house renovations. You have plenty of time to renovate now that the entire world is on hold because of the pandemic. With the number of power tools you have assembled, now your projects are dependent on having a source of electricity. As more people spend more time indoors, energy consumption rises rapidly, causing blackouts in some locations. As a result, power outages might occur in the middle of operations, causing havoc.

SUGGESTIONS FOR PURCHASING HOME POWER TOOLS

There are a few pointers to keep in mind when you shop for new gear. They are as follows:

Purchase Just One Brand of Power Tools

Several companies provide high-quality cordless power tools. They are capable of handling the majority of home-based DIY jobs. However, do not mix and match gadgets from various manufacturers. You will need to transfer batteries from one tool to another. Batteries from multiple brands are not interchangeable. To avoid problems, purchase cordless tools from the same brand.

Invest in High-Quality Cordless Power Tools

Cordless power tools, like any other heavy-duty device, vary in quality from one to the next. As a result, purchasing superior cordless power equipment is a fantastic choice. Certain companies are recognized for producing high-quality tools that can endure for decades. As a result, do extensive study to identify people who provide high-quality tools.

Buy Bare Tools if You Want to Save Money

Typically, big-box retailers offer entirely new, packaged electronics. They are usually fairly pricey. Surprisingly, buying bare tools may save you money. You can purchase tools without batteries from secondhand shops and the internet.

Then, you may replace the batteries in the tool. Doing so will save you money and produce a low-cost set.

Your Toolbox Should Reflect Your Current Level of Expertise

If you're a do-it-yourselfer, your objectives are probably a reflection of your ability level. Most likely, as you gain experience and get better at managing more challenging jobs, you'll want to move up in the project hierarchy. While it may be alluring to get the most cutting-edge gear you come across, you should first determine if your talents and projects necessitate it. Advanced tools only have their full potential when held by a skilled user. For the time being, it's best to limit your purchases to the necessities, such as construction tools you'll use regularly. As your skills in house remodeling and renovation develop, you'll be better able to determine which tools will improve the appearance of your work. And this mindset will allow you to enjoy your projects without filling your home and garage with the latest shiny objects on the store shelves.

5

FASTENERS AND ADHESIVES

Fasteners may be tiny, yet they keep structures upright by connecting the various parts. Woodworking is a skilled trade that needs patience, self-control, and meticulous attention to detail. Its artisans create some of the most durable, aesthetically pleasing, and high-quality items in various sectors.

For businesses such as furniture, cabinets, carpentry, boat design, flooring, framing, and general assembly, industrial woodworking encompasses the manufacture of timber and wood-based goods or materials. The manufacture and assembling of wood-based items necessitate using specifically designed equipment to aid artisans and assembly workers. Examples include:

- Blades and cutting tools.

- Attaching parts like nuts and bolts.
- Industrial-grade adhesives.
- Glue guns.
- Bulk hot melt applicators.

JOINERY AT IT'S BEST

You'll need to bring various items or surfaces closer together and connect them at some point throughout your home remodeling and renovation project to offer strength, provide a particular form, or expand function. You will use a variety of fasteners and adhesives to accomplish this. Let's have a look at what they have to offer.

You Nailed It!

It might be intimidating to go into the nail section of your local hardware shop. These pointy metal parts seem to be almost identical but aren't and presumably have various purposes. Nails are often used to join pieces of wood or lumber but may also be used for other purposes. Nails come in a broad range of shapes, sizes, and designs, making them useful for many purposes. With this in mind, let's look at the various varieties of nails to see which ones are best for particular applications.

The Components of a Nail

Nails come in various shapes and sizes, depending on the material they are driven and the amount of holding strength required. Steel nails are the most common, although stainless steel, iron, copper, aluminum, and bronze may also be used. The tip, shank, and flattened section of a nail are the point, shank, and head, respectively. Common nails and finishing nails are the two primary types of nails. The regular nail has a big, flat head that is driven in flush with the material's surface, making it the most extensively used of all nails.

Finishing nails are typically used for interior paneling and cabinetwork because they provide a cleaner look. A finishing nail has a smaller, narrower head pushed in below the material's surface using a specific tool called a nail set, or punch and then filled in with putty.

If they have a head, nails less than one inch long are called wire nails; if they have a very tiny or no head, they are called brads. Spikes are very thick nails.

Sizes of Nails

The length and gauge of a nail define its size. The letter "d" represents nail length, ranging from 2d to 50d, with comparable lengths.

- 1 inch—2d
- 1 1/4 inch—3d
- 1 1/2 inch—4d
- 1 3/4 inch—5d
- 2 inches—6d

- 2 1/2 inches—8d
- 3 inches—10d
- 3 1/4 inch—12d
- 3 1/2 inch—16d
- 4 inch—20d
- 4 1/2 inch—30d
- 5 inch—40d
- 5 1/2 inch—50d

The diameter of the nail is measured using the nail gauge. The narrower the nail, the higher the gauge. Different nail sizes and gauges are required for other applications. As a general guideline, use a nail that is three times longer than the thickness of the material you're securing.

Common Nails

The most common nail used in construction and building is the common nail, as the name implies. They're a popular option for framing and carpentry work since their thick shank provides dependable support. Instead of being utilized for their aesthetic appeal, these heavy-duty nails are employed for their strength and utility in more tough labor applications. The typical nail's round head is generally visible on surfaces, making it ideal for jobs where function takes precedence.

Framing Nails

Framing nails are durable and lengthy nails used for framing houses or any other woodworking job that needs a solid structure. They are often the same as ordinary nails. Framing nails are smaller and more subtle than regular nails, making them simpler to drive in and maintain flush or even sink for aesthetic purposes.

Box Nails

Box nails resemble regular nails but have a narrower shank, making them less robust and better suited to creating boxes rather than framing buildings. The slimmer shank has the advantage of causing less splitting in thinner pieces of wood. Since they are lighter and weaker than ordinary nails, they are typically employed for lightweight construction. These nails are often galvanized to avoid corrosion.

Sinker Nails

The sinker nail gets its name from its flat, tapering head, enabling it to be driven flush with the wood's surface. Furthermore, the checkered, or grid embossed, head surface inhibits striking hammer slippage. Its vinyl-coated shank offers smooth driving and robust holding strength, making it ideal for general construction, carpentry, and framing tasks.

Roofing Nails

Roofing nails are designated and developed to perform a specific job. Roofing nails are often used to adhere to asphalt and other roofing materials due to their bigger heads and shorter shanks. The big head keeps the thin roof material in place, preventing it from blowing away or being ripped. They're also great for securing house wrap, roof felt, and sheathing. These nails are sometimes slightly bent to boost gripping strength. These nails are generally galvanized to avoid rusting and corrosion since they are continuously exposed to the outdoors.

Masonry Nails

These super-solid, hard nails are usually made of super-tough materials such as steel, and can be driven into masonry surfaces like concrete and brick. This strong nail is often used to join wood to stone or masonry.

Duplex Nails

This kind of nail, often known as double-headed nails, is used in temporary constructions such as scaffolding. This nail features two heads, one above the other, so that when driven into a material, the upper head is still accessible for simple removal after the job is over.

Finishing Nails

Finishing nails are thin, smooth nails that are often employed to complete tasks. They are more aesthetically pleasing due to their neater appearance while still holding any finishing together. Finishing nails are used for trimming, such as down jambs, crown molding, and baseboards because they are lighter and subtler. In the lighter wood often used for finishing work, their slim design also minimizes splitting.

Brad Nails

Brad nails are more subtle than regular nails, making them ideal for jobs that need a polished finish. These nails are thinner than ordinary nails and have smaller heads, making them excellent for reducing splitting and producing a neat look in various woodworking tasks. Nail guns also employ brad nails for rapid repairs and simple attachment.

Drywall Nails

Drywall nails include little rings around the shaft to make them more durable and less prone to snag. They're used to hang gypsum boards and drywall. Many individuals prefer to use drywall screws, which are identical to drywall nails in appearance.

Flooring Nails

Flooring nails are available in several designs, depending on the kind of flooring to be fastened. Some flooring nails include rings that look like screws and are used to join plywood or other subfloors. The coils prevent material from slipping and guarantee that it is firmly connected.

Nails for Use With Nail Guns

One of the most common nails for nail guns is the brad nail. These are commonly referred to as wire nails since they are one of the tiniest nails in the nail family—and because of how thin they are. These will need to be used with a pneumatic or gas-powered finish nailer because of their tiny heads.

Finishing nails are comparable to brad nails and work well with nail guns. These nails are used to complete and complete a product, such as a skirting board or architrave. They're ideal for finishing since they leave a tiny hole that can be filled in or painted over, and they don't leave any residue.

On the other hand, framing nails are more extensive and thicker since they are often used for fastening fires on larger wood constructions such as walls, roofs, and sub-flooring. These work best with a framing nailer, a large-capacity nailer that can handle nails up to 3 1/2 inches long.

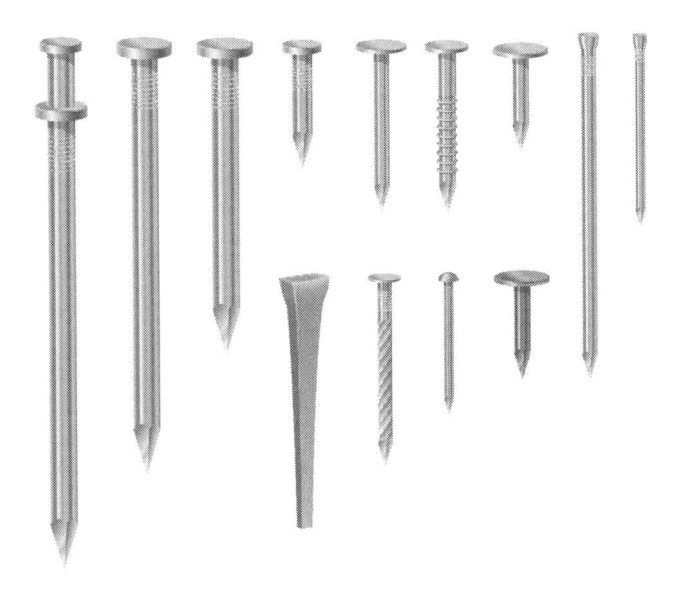

Using Hammer and Nails

Handling a hammer may quickly turn into a game of Russian Roulette with your fingers as the target. When these tools are used, mild-mannered people become unpleasant, with expletives freely streaming from their lips. If you're starting to believe that these ubiquitous household tools are out to harm you, these hammer tips will help you regain control.

Select the Appropriate Hammer for the Task

A blackened nail bed is a foregone conclusion when a little brad nail is driven in with a heavyweight hammer. Attempting to mow the grass with a pair of scissors while using a tack hammer on huge nails is like trying to mow the lawn with a pair of scissors. A medium-weight hammer is your best choice for ordinary home chores. Heavy hammers should be used for framing and driving larger nails into hardwood, while tiny hammers should be used for finishing nails or upholstery tacks. Roughen the nail head with a coarse piece of sandpaper to reduce the likelihood of the hammer sliding.

Hold the nail firmly between your thumb and finger(s) approximately two-thirds of the way up. When you hold the nail too low, it becomes unstable, which increases the chances of it being pushed in at an incorrect angle or damaging your fingers. Use needle-nose pliers to grip nails that are too tiny to grab with a finger.

Lightly Tap the Nail Into the Wood Until It Is Firmly Embedded

By tapping the chisel end of the nail into the wood with the hammer first, you may lessen the chance of breaking the wood. Nails should be driven in at a modest slant.

Get a Good Handle

Swing from the elbow, not the wrist, which should be straight and locked, as you grip the hammer at the bottom of the handle. Keep the handle pointed toward your hips and not to the side of your body. To avoid missing a nail, keep your attention on the nail head at all times.

Set the Nail Using a Nail Set

If you don't have a nail set on hand, substitute another nail by twisting the head sideways and placing it on top of the nail you wish to set. You'll produce indentations on the surface if you don't.

How to Select the Appropriate Screwdriver

Let's move on to picking the correct screwdriver now that you know how to use a hammer. Screws that are stripped are caused by a screwdriver that is too small.

A Screw's Anatomy

Before we go into the varieties, it's essential to understand the critical characteristics to make the best option.

The form of the mechanism that is used to insert and remove screws is known as the drive. Cross-head, square, star, slotted, and hex socket are the most popular drive shapes.

The top of the screw, which contains the drive, is known as the head.

The smooth section of the fastener between the head and the thread is known as the shank. Screws come in a variety of shapes and sizes, and some do not have a smooth shank.

The ridge that wraps around the cylinder and produces a helix is known as the thread.

Selecting the Correct Screw

Screws for Wood

Two wood pieces are joined together using wood screws. You'll require sharp screws with a wedge-shaped shank if you need screws for woodworking. Wood screws come in various lengths, diameters, and drive types and feature a semi-threaded shank. Screws are standard and suitable for most woodworking jobs. When fastening wood, use a screw with a length that will penetrate half the thickness of the bottom material.

Screws for Pocket Holes

Wood is fastened together using pocket hole screws in a pre-drilled pocket hole. Since you can disguise pocket holes, they are often utilized in the construction of furniture and cabinets. They give one of the most secure methods to attach materials when used with a pocket hole jig. There's no need to drill pilot holes before attaching two pieces of fabric since the screw includes a self-tapping head that drills its hole.

Even with a rapidly spinning drill, the square drive of this screw firmly fits a driver and prevents peeling. The square form of the driver makes it unlikely that it will slide out of the screw's hollow head. Since pocket screws are buried within pre-drilled pocket holes, they must be strip-proof because it is tricky to retrieve a stripped screw inside a pocket hole. The flat, washer-style head cushions the wood. It's designed to prevent countersinking and over-drilling in soft materials.

Screws for Drywall

Drywall screws are used to attach drywall to wood or metal studs. They have a coarse thread and a flat tip, making them more straightforward to countersink just below the drywall surface. This feature makes it simple to hide the screw after the drywall is finished. Drywall screws are more durable than drywall nails.

When connecting ordinary 1/2-inch-thick drywall to wood studs, use 1-1/4-inch drywall screws. When installing regular 5/8-inch-thick drywall to ceiling studs, use 1-5/8-inch screws. To give a solid grip, these screw lengths guarantee that the screw drives entirely through the drywall and into at least half the thickness of a standard stud.

Screws for the Deck

Deck screws for outdoor usage are often composed of stainless steel to withstand corrosion. They're also helpful in making planters, window boxes, and outdoor furniture. To reduce the chance of stripping, look for a deck screw with a star head. They can manage a high amount of torque transmission and the force and speed generated by a strong drill.

Screws for Masonry

When attaching items to concrete, mortar joints, and brick, masonry screws are employed. Before inserting a masonry screw, a pilot hole (a tiny hole pre-drilled into the material) must be produced using a carbide bit and a hammer drill. Masonry screws have two heads: a flat head for countersinking and a hex washer head sitting on top of the material's surface.

Screws for Sheet Metal

Metal needs particular fasteners due to its hardness. Sheet metal screws are used to attach and tighten metal components together and affix plastic or wood to metal. Sharp tips and a fine thread run the length of the shank of these screws.

The Difference Between Screws and Bolts

Screws and bolts are the most frequent forms of fasteners. While screws and bolts have some visual similarities, there are a few distinguishing features. In the most basic sense, a screw "screws into" something, while a bolt "bolts things" together. One of the critical distinctions between the two is that a screw fastens directly into the product's surface, but a bolt needs a nut and washer to attach components on the other side of the material.

The tools needed to install the fasteners are another significant distinction between the two. While screws may have various head types, such as slotted, Philips, or square recess heads, you usually won't need extra equipment to insert them if you have the correct screwdriver or drill bit. When fastening components using nuts and bolts, you'll generally need a wrench or driver to tighten the bolt and a second wrench to deliver torque to the nut. A washer is used to disperse the force of the fastener equally.

Screws and Fasteners: How to Use Them

The first step, regardless of the kind of fastener, is to drill a threaded hole in the material that is slightly smaller than the size of the fastener you want to use. Pre-drilling the holes before inserting the fastener will provide a much tighter connection, whether it's a nut or a bolt.

When utilizing threaded fasteners such as screws, be sure you only drill partly through the product's surface so that the screw's threads may adequately catch. After drilling the first hole, you may either continue driving the screw into the material with the drill until the head is flush with the surface or remove the drill and finish the attachment using a manual screwdriver.

When utilizing nuts and bolts, you should drill a clean hole through your material so that your bolt may travel straight through it and connect with a nut on the other end. When choosing bolts for your application, keep in mind the depth of the material you'll be attaching since you don't want the bolt to be too short or too long to make the connection.

Bolts and Nuts

Bolts are threaded fasteners typically used in conjunction with a threaded nut to attach two or more components. Bolts are divided into many varieties based on their head forms, strengths, finishes, and materials. These categories all play a part in determining which bolt type is best for a given application. Because numerous bolt designs are more effective than others, it is essential to have the necessary information to pick the best bolt type for a particular work.

Bolt Types and Applications

The heads of bolts and screws come in a wide range of forms. The purpose of these heads is to hold the tools that are used to tighten them. Bolt heads come in various shapes and sizes, including square, hex, slotted hex washer, and socket cap.

Square heads were the first bolt heads to be used. Square heads are made out of a square depression on the head and a shaft that can resist rotation when torque is applied. Hex heads have grown increasingly popular in recent years. However, square heads are still in use. You will use a wrench or a spanner to create torque on bolts with hexagonal heads. Flat, oval, pan, round, button, and truss are some of the different head forms used.

Bolts for Anchoring

Use: Light poles, structural beams, and equipment fastening to the concrete are all applications. Bolts that have a threaded end and a non-threaded L-shaped end are used for anchoring. A washer and a nut are usually included—and rust-resistant construction.

Bolts With Toggles

It's also known as a butterfly anchor—shafts with entire threads and a nut in the form of an expanding wing.

Use: Hanging bulky items in drywall and plaster.

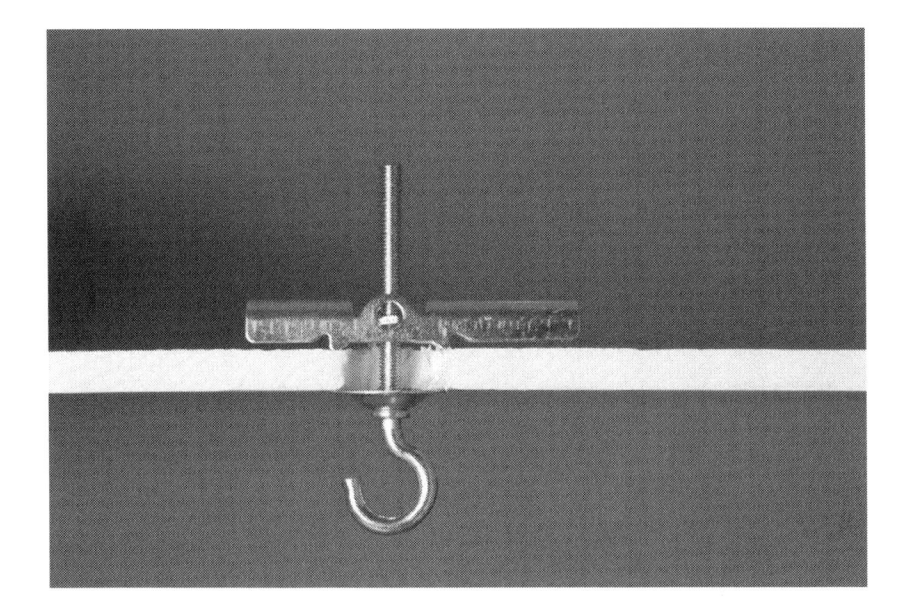

U-bolts

Both ends are threaded in the shape of the letter U.

Use: To support pipework, particularly pipes that carry liquids and gases.

Understanding Adhesives and Glues

Adhesive PVA

Since it works so well in various wood applications, this is often referred to as "woodworker's glue." Interior, Water-resistant, and Waterproof versions are also offered. A clamp will come in helpful for most projects to guarantee that the bonded surfaces make a firm connection. It's ideal not to use too much glue and apply it to only one of the surfaces at a time since this will prevent glue beads from seeping out on the sides after the surfaces are squeezed together.

Epoxy Adhesive

Gloves are required for this glue since the substance warms up once combined. Two-part epoxy adhesives, as well as a dual-tube 5-minute setting option, are available. A decent rule of thumb for blending the two-part mixing epoxy is to start with one part Hardener and two parts Resin. Make sure you read the manufacturer's directions. Ensure the glue is well mixed.

Super Glue

Super Glue is the most common household glue, and you can use it for various non-load bearing applications.

Contact Adhesive

Most of these adhesives, also known as Rubber or Contact Cement, are water and heat resistant and adhere instantaneously. These adhesives are ideal for bonding non-porous materials (such as glass, metals, plastic) and do not need clamping.

Adhesive for Wall Tiles

When dealing with non-porous tiles, such as porcelain, it's ideal to utilize a powder-based adhesive with a chemical drying process that doesn't necessitate water loss. This glue is available in both powder and cement forms. Water that cannot entirely escape from the back of the tile is bound by the drying chemical, ensuring a good bond between the tile and the wall.

Threadlocker

This glue is used to keep nuts and washers firmly attached to the threads of screws and bolts so they don't come undone. It's available in various strengths, so be sure you know which one you'll need for your project.

Adhesive Made of Polyurethane

These adhesives can be used on porous and non-porous surfaces, but they won't stick to Teflon, silicone, waxy, or greasy surfaces. This glue can be set in high moisture environments, making it ideal for repairing boats. It can also be sanded, stained, and painted over and has good UV resistance. The product may be safe to eat after it has been cured. The items you're gluing together with this glue must fit together securely. In arid conditions, the product will need pre-wetting of the surfaces to set correctly.

Nail Polish in Liquid Form

Interior and heavy-duty versions of this glue are available. It's simple to wash away with water. It also has a flexible and impact-resistant bond, making it suitable for use with wood. Cabinets, countertops, brick veneers, and a variety of other modest building projects may all benefit from the heavy-duty option. Check the box carefully since there are a variety of distinct types with varied applications.

Sealant vs. Caulk

With so many different caulks and sealants to choose from, it's easy to get overwhelmed when it comes to selecting the right product for your next bathroom or kitchen renovation. Both chemicals have the same function: Sealing agents to cover gaps and cracks and bonding agents between construction components like countertops and sink bases. Both are applied to surfaces using a caulking gun to prevent leaks, which is why a sealant is officially classified as a sort of caulk.

When to Apply Silicone Sealant

A silicone sealer that is 100 percent silicone adheres to porcelain, ceramic, marble, fiberglass, and most metals. It's perfect for damp, outdoor applications since it's weather-resistant and includes antibacterial characteristics that prevent mold and mildew development. The sealant is also UV-resistant, preventing yellowing and extending the life of a seal when exposed to direct sunshine. Silicone sealant dries quickly, hardening entirely in only 24 hours.

Silicone sealants are ideal for kitchen and bath applications because of their high adhesiveness, flexibility, and water resistance.

- Countertops with top mount and under-mount

- Surrounds for bathtubs, showers, doors, and drains
- Gaps and seams in gutters
- Nail or screw holes on the outside
- HVAC-related applications

When to Use a Caulk That Is Both Acrylic and Latex

Water-based acrylic-latex caulk, often known as latex or general-purpose caulk, adheres well to most common construction materials, including wood. Once cured, it is paintable, creates fewer fumes, and can be wiped up with light soap and water rather than a chemical solvent, unlike silicone sealants.

Tub-N-Tile caulk is a specialist acrylic-latex caulk with an improved mildewcide that prevents mildew development in moist environments. This form of caulk is also simpler to apply, making it excellent for difficult-to-reach or time-sensitive jobs. However, acrylic-latex caulks only give a modest amount of water resistance, so they're better suited for indoor applications where they won't be exposed to water regularly. It might take up to 72 hours for acrylic-latex caulks to harden fully.

Regular and specialty acrylic-latex caulk is often used in the following plumbing applications

- keeping loose tiles in place
- bathtubs, showers, sinks, and toilets
- crown molding and baseboards

- gaps surrounding plumbing fittings

When to Use Hybrid Caulk: Siliconized Acrylic-Latex

Choose a siliconized acrylic latex caulk if you want to combine the strong sealing capabilities of a silicone sealant with the ease of application and cleanup of an acrylic-latex caulk. The hybrid caulk creates a watertight barrier that won't crumble or shrink as the temperature changes, making it flexible and long-lasting. It's also designed to dry rapidly (in only 24 hours) and slide easily over surfaces for hassle-free sculpting and blending.

- surrounds for the bathtub and shower
- backsplashes
- exterior siding sealing
- reducing drafts via windows and doors

The temperature range and moisture level at the application location are the two most critical aspects to consider when choosing a caulk or sealant. Since it is mainly silicone, a sealant has better flexibility and water resistance. As temperatures change, the silicone substance permits a sealant to stretch and shrink without breaking its airtight or watertight barrier. As a result, sealants are an excellent solution for places with high moisture levels and frequent weather changes, such as kitchens and bathrooms and around doors and windows.

6

STARTING WITH DOORS AND WINDOWS

The glass installer you pick may employ technical terms if you're thinking about replacing or upgrading your home's windows. A window has more parts than you think, and it's good to know what a glass expert could include in their estimates. Many do-it-yourselfers are successful in completing their window replacement tasks. From appraising the task and learning the vocabulary to installing your replacement windows like an expert, here's how to become one of them.

WINDOWS

The amount of expertise required to replace your windows varies based on the sort of repair job. A full-frame replacement window, for example, is more challenging to install than an insert replacement window. A full-frame replacement window involves a complete tear-out and replacement of the current one. Still, an insert replacement window enables you to preserve the original window frame and trim. Reviewing the product installation instructions or watching our installation videos is a brilliant place to start when assessing the scope of a replacement job.

An External View of a Window

The external anatomy of a window is divided into

Frame

The frame surrounds and supports the window system. It has a head, a jam, and a sill.

Head

The head is the principal horizontal component that creates the window frame's top.

Jambs

On the top of the window frame, the head jamb is the horizontal component, and the side jambs are the principal vertical components that form the sides.

Sill

The sill is the principal horizontal component of the window frame. Its exterior is tapered to assist it in shedding water.

Jamb Liner

The jamb liner is a strip that goes between the window frame and the inner wall. It's commonly made of wood and can be installed during manufacturing or while replacing windows. The structure may be plastered or drywalled to remove the need for a jamb liner.

Interior Window Anatomy

Components of a window's interior anatomy include:

Sash

The sash is the window's moveable component that secures the glass. Some materials include wood, vinyl, fiberglass, aluminum, and composite. Two sashes tilt inward and slide up and down in a double-hung window. Comparable to a casement window, sliding windows have one sash that glides from left to right.

Stile

Stiles are the vertical sash portions.

Rail

Rails are the horizontal sash parts.

Check Rail

Each glass pane's frame meets a check rail. The check rails meet at the middle of a double-hung window or where the bottom sash (top check rail) completes the top cash rail (bottom check rail). A sliding window's check rails are where the two vertical panes of glass meet.

Top Rail

The top rail is the visible section of the top sash.

Bottom Railing

The lower rail is the lowest portion of the lower sash.

Glazing

The glass within the window frame is called glazing. Modern windows include two or three layers of glass with an inert gas pushed between them for further insulation. Invisible window coatings can alter how much light and heat pass through or reflect off them. Tinted or laminated glass may provide privacy and strength.

Lift

A lift is a handle that raises the bottom sash of a wooden window.

Sash Pin Tilt

The sash tilt pin allows sashes to tilt inwards to clean the exterior of the panes from inside the home.

Sash Lock

The sash lock's locking mechanism touches the window's lock strike to decrease rattling.

Balances

Window balances are devices that counterbalance the sashes of a single-hung or double-hung window to make them easier to open and shut. These days, they're manufactured using block and tackle systems that employ strings to produce tension.

Handle

The operational handle on the casement or awning windows opens and shuts the sash using the operating arm. A crank working handle extends the operating arm and opens the sash; it retracts and closes it. You can manually open and close specific windows using non-crank handles.

Working Arm

The working arm on the casement, awning, and hopper windows works with the operating handle to open and close the sash.

Locked Handle

The locking handle brings the sashes together to promote energy efficiency and security.

Window Materials

Single-sash window: A single sash window opens from the bottom. Open single-hung windows are flush with the wall.

Two-sash window: A window that has two operable sashes on each side. Double-hung windows open flush against the wall.

Check Rail: The check rail is the piece of a double-hung window where the upper and lower sashes meet (the middle of the window).

Glass Types

Different glass or window styles are described as follows.

Insulated Glass Windows

Components like argon (a kind of gas) can make windows more energy efficient. Their other term is double-pane windows.

PVC Windows Vinyl

These windows are framed with PVC Vinyl rather than wood, metal, or fiberglass. This kind of window is low-maintenance and will last a long time.

Laminated Glass

Hard to fracture glass. A glass window with lamination prevents it from breaking into fragments.

Tempered Glass

This kind of safety glass is similar to laminated glass in that it is heat toughened.

Low-E Glass

Low-E Glass is a low-emissivity glass that reflects heat. This kind of coated glass removes the need for tinted windows.

The Best Window for Your Location

Choosing windows is more complex than choosing a style. Windows in different regions of the country will operate and age differently. Here's a list of things to watch for and avoid depending on your location.

Northwest

Residents in the Pacific Northwest like their views, so choosing windows with plenty of glass while remaining energy efficient is crucial. Vinyl, wood-resin composite, and fiberglass are excellent moisture-resistant window materials. Because summers in this location are moderate and short, use windows with a higher solar heat gain coefficient.

Southwest

This location has a moderate summer temperature and a cold winter climate. Insulating windows are essential. To avoid the sun's beams, look for windows with a solar heat gain coefficient (SHGC) of less than 0.3.

Midwest

Heavy rains, severe gusts, and the potential of tornadoes make this place risky. During the winter, it may be exceedingly chilly. In the southern and central Midwest, SHGC and

U-values of 0.3 or less might assist. Window experts advise homeowners in windy areas to have casement windows because they perform better in strong winds.

Southeast

Solar-blocking windows lessen the workload on your air conditioner and your summer electricity bill. A basic double-paned, gas-filled vinyl window should suffice in this climate.

SE Coastal

Hurricane resistance and strict window restrictions are significant issues here. Storms may damage a property's structural integrity by removing windows and doors. Impact, structural pressure, air, and water leakage resistance are now needed.

Replacing a Broken Window

Step 1: Remove the shattered glass. You may then wrap up the shards of glass and dispose of them by placing them on the large piece of plastic set on each side of the pane (inside or outside of a window). Using a lot of masking tape to hold the larger pieces together is a good idea.

Step 2: Remove the old putty from the window frame using a putty knife or a wood chisel. Make sure all the old putty is gone.

Step 3: Remove all glazier's points, tiny metal triangles hammered into the frame beneath the putty to hold the glass in place.

Step 4: Apply a thick coating of linseed oil to the frame to prevent drying the putty's oil. Soaking the wood in water makes the putty more pliable and lasts longer.

Step 5: Put very thin beading around the frame where the new glass will be inserted to cushion the glass.

Replacing the Pane

Step 1: Insert the new windowpane with care. Keeping one hand on the glass, firmly press it down and insert a glazier's point on each side to secure it.

Step 2: Install glazier's points every 100mm along each edge.

Step 3: Apply the putty like a dry, thick dough. You can use the manufacturer's recommended thinner. Cut the putty into pencil-sized strips and wrap them around the window.

Step 4: After applying the putty, smooth it out with long, even strokes. The putty should finish smooth and level at a 30-45° angle to the glass. It shouldn't be visible from inside the window.

Step 5: Run the knife inside the frame to remove excess putty and create a neat edge.

Preventing Window Shatters

Window Film Protection

Window security films are a low-cost option for window protection. They attach to existing windows and prevent them from breaking, thus protecting you. Window protection films reduce glare from the sun and can tint windows to keep curious eyes out. Some are made of steel, making it difficult to break them even with brute force. So they keep your home safe from intruders. You can also use these films to create a one-way effect for your property.

Use Tempered Glass

If you're thinking about replacing your windows, tempered glass can be a good option. They are tough to break, which deters robbers. They disintegrate rather than shatter into thousands of pieces when shattered. To increase its strength, this kind of glass goes through repeated heating and cooling steps.

Transparent Plastic Film

A transparent plastic film is layered between two glasses in this kind of protective window pane. When pressured, the film is highly robust, resists tearing, and may stretch. The film remains intact when either side of the glass is cracked. Nothing or no one will be able to enter your home using this strategy. When it rains, it even keeps water from flooding your home.

Cleaning and Maintaining Your Windows

No matter how frequently you clean the windows, dirt and debris will eventually collect. As a result, you must clean them regularly to keep them gleaming.

Clean the Window Frame

Always wipe the window sills and frame before beginning to clean the window glass. The liquid will leak over the frame during the cleaning, resulting in a muddy mess. It has the potential to sabotage your cleaning efforts. After vacuuming the frame, start cleaning the glass surface. Even after properly washing the glass, residual residue may form in the window panes' corners. Use cotton swabs to remove these deposits since you can't wipe them with a cloth or a squeegee.

Make Use of a Sponge

If you wipe the glass with an old t-shirt or a towel, you won't be able to achieve sparkling clean windows. Window panes may be cleaned using a microfiber cloth or a squeegee. Window glass may also be cleansed using newspaper sheets. You won't have to worry about stains since glass doesn't absorb ink from paper.

Use Distilled Water

You have the option of purchasing a window cleaning solution from a shop or making your own. Always use pure water when diluting vinegar cleaning solutions. Many individuals use tap water for this reason, so streaks on the glass surface are a problem. Since tap water contains contaminants, it creates tenacious stains even when using high-quality tools. You can clean window glass more successfully with distilled water.

Use strong vinegar if the glass is murky and you haven't cleaned it in a while. Fill a spray bottle halfway with warm vinegar and squirt it all over the windows. Allow the solution to sit for a minute or two before wiping it clean with a paper towel.

Make Sure You Have Enough of Cleaning Solution

Some individuals clean their windows using a little bit of cleaning solution. As a consequence, the solution falls short of dissolving the dirt and particles, leaving streaks behind. As a result, liberally apply the cleaning solution to the windows. The cleaning solution can successfully remove stains and debris from even the dirtiest window panes and clean them.

Screens That Keep Insects at Bay

Installing screens in windows and doors is a terrific method to keep pests at bay. To keep out the most prevalent creepy crawlies, go for a 20-mesh or finer mesh. Bugs may also get through existing screens that have holes or rips in them. Carefully put the damaged wires back into place using a screwdriver or scissors.

Apply a layer of transparent nail paint to the hole to seal it and keep insects out. If the screen has come free along one side or corner, reattach it to the frame using staples (for wood frames) or a splining tool (for aluminum frames). If these fast repairs aren't working, give Blue Springs Siding and Windows or similar windows contractors a call for a free screen door evaluation.

Inspecting and Repairing Casement Windows

As a consequence of gravity, a casement window will progressively sag over time, and it only takes a few millimeters of drop for the window to start catching against the frame. If your window is dragging, you'll need to compensate by adjusting the hinge channel. Adjust it from the outside. You'll need to figure out which way your window is drooping and then adjust the relevant hinge.

Step 1: Start by removing the arms that make up the bottom of the window's hinge. Unscrew everything and open it up. The sash that is tethered to the window frame may then be lifted out.

Step 2: Now, it's time to fill in the gaps. If your windows are uPVC, use epoxy resin; if they're wood, use wood filler. Don't miss this step since you'll be drilling new holes within a few centimeters from the old ones, and the drill might become stuck in the old ones. To get the greatest possible finish, be sure to massage the filler smooth.

Step 3: Now, you'll use a ⅛-inch pilot drill to drill some new holes. Drill them a few millimeters more expensive than the original holes. Given that there's no way to test the window before it's fastened to the frame, a little guessing may be necessary. If you've just recently become aware of the issue, a slight adjustment to the hinge will likely provide a significant improvement.

Repair a Shattered Window

Broken glass windows may be sealed using solvent-based adhesives like epoxy. While you wait for a replacement, it's a wonderful technique to keep the glass intact and avoid more damage for an extended period. These steps will show you how to use epoxy to repair shattered windows.

You'll need the following items:

- dishwashing liquid soap
- cleaner for windows
- cotton rags or microfiber fabric
- knife for epoxy putty
- plate made of paper
- acetone

Step 1: To remove any dust, fingerprints, or oil residue, clean the glass section of the window using liquid dishwashing detergent and a moist microfiber cloth. Allow for a few minutes for it to dry entirely.

Step 2: Combine the hardener and the resin to make a two-part epoxy mixture. On a disposable cardboard or paper plate, mix and combine the solution with a toothpick.

Step 3: Apply the epoxy mixture to the shattered glass using a putty knife, carefully pushing to fill up the fractures. Allow at least five minutes for it to dry.

Step 4: Using a sharp blade or a few drops of acetone on cotton or a dry cloth, remove any excess epoxy that has protruded on the surface.

Step 5: Using a glass cleaner and a clean cloth, polish your glass window.

Replacing Storm Windows

Remove the Storm Window Panes

Step 1: Pull in on the lowest corner springs to remove the glass from the window. If the plastic clips are damaged, use a flat-bladed screwdriver to push them in.

Step 2: After the springs have been pushed all the way in, swing the bottom of the window in toward you.

Step 3: About halfway up the window, lower the top of the window until the corner pegs connect with the release holes in the sides of the window frame. Pull the corner pegs out of the slots using your fingers. By reversing the removal process, you may reinstall the pane.

Replacing Spring Clips and Pins

Step 1: Remove the glass from the frame. Make that both springs are working correctly. Remove any spring clips that aren't sliding in readily and bounce them back into place. To release the clip, press up against the small nylon square protruding through the bottom of the frame. Slide it out the spring slide's other end, taking care not to lose the spring.

Step 2: Replace the small plastic pin on the spring's inside end. Place the spring on top of it and slide the new clip into place from the spring's outer end. The small nylon square tab will snap into the hole in the bottom of the frame to keep it in place. Check to see if the spring is working correctly.

Step 3: Look for any cracks or weaknesses in the top pegs. Look for the small rectangle indentations that hold the pin in place about an inch from the corner to remove the corner pins. Drill a hole through the indentation with a 3/16-inch bit to release the pressure and slide the pin out.

Step 4: Insert a new pin from the corner and tap it firmly against the outside edge until it's flush. To indent the frame, firmly tap the tip of a little, flat-blade screwdriver into it, a little closer to the corner than the hole where the original intent was.

Replacing Cracked Glass

Step 1: Remove the glass and both top corner pegs. Remove the top piece of the frame and carefully pull out the side parts, taking care not to go any farther than is necessary to remove the shattered glass.

Step 2: Measure the pane from top to bottom and side to side. Purchase replacement glass that is 3/8 inch higher and broader than the frame's interior measurements.

Step 3: Remove the shattered glass from the frame, as well as the rubber seal that folds over the frame's edge. Apply the rubber seal around the new pane's edges. Insert the sealed glass into the frame's groove, pushing the side pieces back into place and fixing the top piece. Replace the corner pins if necessary.

Installing a Window: A Step-by-Step Guide

Step 1: To mark the corners of the window, drive nails through the wall from within the home. Then, on the exterior, draw a window opening.

Step 2: Use a power saw to cut through the siding and sheathing, being careful to use the right blade. Check the fit of the window by bringing it up to the opening. If necessary, keep cutting.

Step 3: To make sure the window will fit, place it in the opening. Make sure the aperture is a little bigger than the actual window. If necessary, cut through the siding and drywall again to make more room. To find out how much space you should allow, see the manufacturer's instructions.

Step 4: Tuck 8-inch-wide pieces of moisture seal into the siding to line the opening. With a utility knife, slit the corners of the moisture seal diagonally and fold the pieces toward the inside. If required, trim the strips until they are slightly within the opening's inner edge. Then staple them together, starting at the bottom and working your way up.

Step 5: Place two tiny 1/2-inch spacers in the bottom of the aperture, approximately 1/2 inch in from the sides, at this stage. Check for level and, if necessary, apply shims. To attach the shims to the aperture, use dabs of silicone or two 6d (2-inch) nails per pair (if you use nails, pre-drill nail holes). Cut them flush with the siding once they've been fastened.

Installing a Window

Place the bottom of the window on the spacers from outside the house. And then carefully slide the top into the opening. Ensure it's the correct way up; there may be drained holes at the bottom that prevent moisture from escaping.

At one of the higher corners, drive a nail halfway through the trim. Check the window level, make any required shim adjustments, and then continue driving the nail. Recheck the level. Then walk inside and double-check that everything is in order from that angle. Nail the other corners and then around the perimeter.

Secure the Flange Once You've Positioned the Window

Install shims along the edges of the window towards the top and bottom and in the middle, and adjust as required until the window is plumb. Ensure the window is functional before securing it to the aperture with nails driven into the brick mold or casing. Follow the manufacturer's directions for applying flashing and sealant (both outside and inside).

Put the Window Together

Apply the trim to the window's exterior and caulk the gap between the window and the siding as directed by the manufacturer. Check the window for level inside and apply shims along the sides until it fits snugly in the opening.

Finally, nail through the jamb and the shims into the trimmer studs with 8d (2 1/2-inch) finishing nails; use a nail set to set the nailheads slightly below the surface. Add insulation between the jambs and the trimmer studs, cut the shims level with the wall, and attach the inside trim. The window frame should be shimmed and fastened. Molding may be used to finish your project on the inside.

DOORS

It does not have to be challenging to choose the correct interior door type for your house. There are several elements at work, but it becomes a lot less daunting when narrowed down. Your interior doors will have a significant impact on the decor and flow of your house.

Types of Doors

Bi-Fold Doors

Bi-fold doors fold shut inside the door frame, saving space on a typical door. The door does not open into or out of the chamber; instead, the two pieces fold left or right. There is no track on the floor and a pivot hinge on the frame, so there are no risks or impediments for children or wheelchair users.

Engineered Doors

The most prevalent form of mass-produced door is the engineered door. Solid strips or blocks of lumber are bonded together and coated with a decorative varnish or veneer to achieve an appealing final finish. Various thicknesses and materials may be employed. A thick piece of wood around the exterior as lipping can match the door grain. Because of panel matching, engineered doors are frequently more consistent in their wood appearance.

French Doors

Also known as double doors, they are a pair of doors with hinges that open outwards. Due to the dramatic impact of these doors and the fact that they often have a lot of glass, they're mainly used between dining rooms and living rooms and onto patio areas. There are several finishes, materials, and styles from which to choose.

Flush Doors

Flush doors are flat, basic doors with no decorative elements on either side. They're attractive and straightforward, with high-quality manufacturing and varnishes available to provide a variety of distinct final finishes.

Hardwood Doors

Due to the timber used to make them, hardwood doors are thick, sturdy, and long-lasting. Hardwood is more resistant to decay, and since it is more robust, it is more suited for usage outside than softwood. Because of the wood, external hardwood doors may have a gorgeous high-density grain finish. Hardwoods that are often used include beech, walnut, mahogany, and oak.

Room Dividers

A room divider is a pair of interior doors between two rooms or an inner porch entrance.

Sidelights

Sidelight is a transparent, opaque, or stained sheet of glass located on the side of a door frame that adds elegance to an entryway. Sidelights are typical for outdoor front doors and maybe single-sided or double-sided, depending on the side of the door where you have room.

Sliding Glass Doors

Sliding doors open by sliding sideways within a room opening. This door style is a valuable space-saver for busy family homes, particularly if every bit of floor space is required or where a door leading into the room would clash with furniture. Sliding doors, often known as pocket doors, may glide on a track across a wall or into a hollow in the wall.

Stable Doors

Due to their construction, stable doors are most typically seen leading to and from a kitchen. These doors split in half and maybe opened from either the top or bottom. Stable doors are ideal for allowing air into a kitchen while keeping youngsters and dogs out.

Save Energy: Installing Weatherstripping and Door Sweeps

Weatherstripping is a low-cost and straightforward approach to increasing a home's energy efficiency by minimizing air leaks via doors and operable windows by sealing the moving connections when the door or window is closed, giving excellent protection against air drafts.

Some new doors may come with factory-applied weatherstripping, but the efficiency of this stripping may deteriorate with time, causing air leaks to reappear. On the other hand, many doors and windows have little to no weatherstripping or weatherstripping that no longer operates as effectively as it once did.

V-Strip

This style of weatherstripping is constructed of metal or vinyl and consists of a big strip of material folded back along itself. This kind is more sturdy, long-lasting, and simple to install, making it ideal for retrofitting older houses. Many are self-adhesive and may be pushed along the frame without the need for tools. More costly bronze versions give a better seal, but you must nail them into place.

Felt

This felt-based weatherstripping comes in rolls that are cut and stapled into place, and it may be simple or reinforced with a thin metal strip. These must be fitted in such a way that the seal pushes against them. These strips are pretty sensitive, need to be replaced every one to two years, and cannot be utilized in locations where they will be exposed to moisture or extreme abrasion. This sort of weatherstripping is quite apparent when installed.

Sweep

This seal is aluminum or stainless steel with a plastic, vinyl, sponge, or felt brush. The sweep is placed to the bottom side of a door to prevent drafts from coming in. A door sweep is quite simple to install, and you may order many versions accommodate an uneven door.

How to Change a Doorknob

You will need

- screwdriver
- safety glasses
- door knob hardware kit

Make sure you properly remove your old doorknob before installing your new one.

Replace the Latch Plate

Place the new doorknob latch on the inside of the door. The rotating lock's tapered side should face the striking plate on the door frame. Use the included screws to secure the new lock plate.

Replace the Knob and Spindle

A long spindle will be affixed to the outside of the knob. Pass this through the lock you just inserted. The spindle will now be visible on the opposite side of the door. On the inner side of the door, secure it with a plate and the given hardware.

Finish by Attaching the Inside Knob

The inner handle should be able to slip freely over the spindle. Align the components and secure them in place. Our new knob included a concealed set screw that needed to be tightened using a long Allen wrench that came with the doorknob. To ensure that everything is in place, test the new doorknob.

Repair Typical Door Issues

If you need to repair any doors, here are some fast and straightforward ways to get you started.

Trouble Closing the Door

The latch bolt will be out of line with the striking plate if the door sags slightly. You may correct slight misalignment by unscrewing the plate and widening the cut-out with a tiny metal file. Alternatively, remove the striking plate and secure it lower down the frame. Extend the depression into which it fits using a sharp chisel and a hammer. Dowels can fill in the old screw holes if the plate only moves a short distance. Drill fresh pilot holes for the screw fixings.

Repair a Sagging Door Frame

Slamming a door often causes the frame to become loose.

Step 1: Make new fixings for brick walls by using three easy-drive Fischer wall anchors on each side of the frame. The frame plugs, which come with hammer-in screws, should be at least 2 ⅓ inches longer than the thickness of the frame.

Step 2: Put a drill bit through the frame and into the wall behind it to the desired depth, using the suitable size masonry bit for the size of the wall plug you will be using.

Step 3: Slamming a door often causes the frame to become loose. Make new fixings for brick walls by using three easy-drive Fischer wall anchors on each side of the frame.

Step 4: Hammer the screw into the hole and insert the plug until the screw head is flush with the frame.

Unable to Close the Door

A hinge-bound door is difficult to shut and tends to spring open. The issue is frequently caused by hinge recesses carved too deeply into the door edge or the frame.

When properly installed, the hinge flaps should be level with the surface of the wood. Protruding screw heads and improperly positioned hinge flaps may prevent a door from closing and potentially cause damage to the door.

Open the door completely before inserting a wedge under it. Remove the hinge screws after cleaning any paint from the slots. Starting with the bottom hinges, remove the screws, leaving at least one screw connected to the top hinge until last. Then have someone hold the door open while you remove the last screw.

Hinges may bind if the screws are installed incorrectly, or their heads are too large for the hinge flap countersinks. Discard troublesome screws and replace them with smaller-headed screws. Pack out the holes with matches, toothpicks, and wood glue if they won't tighten.

Binding may also be caused by hinge flaps that are too close to the doorstop or rebate. The face pushes against the stop as the door closes. Remove the hinges, drill out the existing screw holes, and fill them with glued dowels. Remove the dowel ends and chisel them flush with the cavity.

Drill new fixing holes to move the hinge away from the doorstop. The hinge pin should be slightly visible above the door's edge. Use wood filler to fill the gaps left by the relocated hinges.

Choosing a Casing Style for Your House

Door casings are available in various styles, ranging from elaborate and exquisite to clean and straightforward—something there's for everyone's taste. You should maintain the trim similar from room to room for flow and consistency.

Typically, door trim mirrors window trim style—sizes vary depending on the home's many aspects. For example, apply the most detailed and expansive trim to the inside side of the front entrance door; the next biggest trim should be used to the inner side of other large external doors, such as french and sliding doors; the next biggest trim should be used to the inner side of other large external doors, such as french and sliding doors.

Farmhouse

Farmhouse door casings provide a warm touch to your property. Simple, clean lines with minimal to no embellishment on the boards define timeless farmhouse design. Try whitewashing, staining, or painting your farmhouse-style door casings to give character and depth to a space.

Craftsman

Craftsman door casings are subtle but intriguing accents that lend a purposeful design to your house. Craftsman-style door casings' robust quality and handmade parts also play an essential function in complementing and integrating the outside elements. Paint the door casings a creamy neutral tone or a dark hue to give depth and dimension to your craftsman's house.

Minimal

Minimalist door trim creates a basic, completed, and clean appearance without overpowering the room. Minimal trimming works well with modern or industrial décor types and casual settings to give contemporary interiors a sophisticated and open atmosphere.

Colonial

Colonial-style door casings mix timeless simplicity and rich features to create a sense of warmth and comfort in your house. They may make a low-ceiling space appear more feminine and spacious by integrating magnetic, simple beads and cavetto (concave) forms and curves in their design.

How to Install an Entryway Door

In general, if you have basic carpentry abilities, you should replace both interior and exterior doors on your own. It may be a terrific weekend project for do-it-yourselfers but bear in mind that a professional can make quick work of such a task. In many circumstances, it may be the wisest decision to assure correct completion. And, as we constantly say, what is the value of your time?

Also, if you are not comfortable dealing with power tools or lack fundamental home renovation abilities, you might consider hiring a professional. In most cases, asking for installation advice at the shop where you purchased the door is the quickest method to discover someone competent. Many home improvement businesses have already partnered with qualified specialists to supply you with these services.

Inside Doors

If you've determined you can install your doors, here are step-by-step instructions to help you get started.

Step 1: Slide the pins out and raise the door free to remove the old door. Make sure someone is holding the door open while you remove the pins.

Step 2: Take off the door's hinges. Set them aside if they are in excellent shape to be used on the new entry.

Step 3: Create a pattern using the old door and lay the new door precisely on top of it. If required, trim the bottom of the door to ensure it is the same height as the old one, using the old door as a reference. Trim the door using a fine tooth saw.

Step 4: Create mortises in the new door—mortises are the areas on the edge of the door cut out to enable the hinge to rest level. Mark the new door where the hinge mortises should go using the existing door as a template. Now, trace the precise location of the mortise with the actual old hinge.

Step 5: Using a very sharp wood chisel, score the mortise outline to a depth equal to the hinge. Remove any extra wood with a chisel, then verify the depth with a door hinge. Reattach the door hinge with wood screws after the required depth has been obtained.

Step 6: Use the template and instructions that came with the knob to install it. If necessary, use the same mortising process described above to install a new striking plate.

Step 7: Replace the door pins and hang the door. Check for appropriate fit and trim the door if needed.

Outside Doors

With a few differences, installing an external door is almost identical to that of an interior door.

For starters, you may wish to add a lock and a peephole for security. Second, to avoid moisture damage and warping, make sure a new outside wood door is professionally painted, stained, or sealed. These solutions will come with thorough installation instructions and can be purchased at any home improvement shop.

Increase the Security of Your Front Entrance

If a home invader or thief is determined to enter your house, merely shutting the doors may not be sufficient. A door erected by a builder using standard equipment is surprisingly simple to dismantle with a few strong kicks. If you want to make your house safer against break-ins, you should reinforce your doors.

Smart Locks

For the forgetful homeowner, smart locks are the answer. Many smart locks enable you to unlock the door with a code. Smart locks may also assist you if you fail to lock the doors. Many smart locks may be configured to lock at a particular time of day or after being left unlocked for an extended time. This automatic lock action means that your house will remain safe even if you are late for work and fail to shut the door behind you.

Strengthen the Door Frame and Jamb

While a reinforced strike plate makes it much more difficult for a thief to enter your house, an attacker may ultimately be able to fracture or pull away from the door frame itself with enough effort. To avoid this, you should strengthen the door frame itself. Many firms provide items that add a layer of steel to the door frame to prevent separating. These items are simple to install and will blend in with the doorframe. With only a few screws, you can make the task of kicking down the door considerably more difficult.

Make Use of a Door Barricade

Door barriers and security bars are both additional pieces of hardware that will increase the protection of your door. Consider them supplementary locks, which are likely more robust and resistant to kicks than your present ones. You do not have to choose between a security bar and a door barrier. They are put at various locations on the door, and when combined, they make an entrance practically impregnable. Furthermore, they aren't necessarily substituted for enhancing your strike plate or deadbolt, but instead additional upgrades. When you start stacking defenses, that's when you begin to tighten up your home's protection.

7

THE SPARKS OF RENOVATION—ELECTRICAL PROJECTS

Electrical wiring may be challenging, particularly for the inexperienced. That is why, unless the task is easy, it is typically advisable to engage a professional. Otherwise, you risk injury, property damage, or fire. If you want to finish a DIY project that includes an electrical component, there are several fundamental concepts to understand about wire installation.

THE FUNDAMENTALS OF ELECTRICAL WIRING

Every residence has a power meter from the utility company, then a master 200-amp circuit breaker, and ultimately a breaker box, which is still referred to as a fuse box.

The breaker box sends electricity to different parts of the home through separate circuit breakers, which prevent the system from overloading. Except for certain essential items like an electric dryer, which requires 240 volts, a home's electrical system is designed to run on 120 volts.

Home Wire Types

Three wires in an insulated sleeve is a standard household electrical wire. The "hot" wire is a black wire that conducts electricity. The "neutral" wire is white, while the "ground" wire is bare copper. The black wires must be linked to the black wires, the white wires to the white wires, and the ground wires must be connected. The circuit will not work otherwise, causing an electrical "short."

Black wire is used in applications that need an additional "hot" wire, such as three-way switches. Three-conductor wiring contains white neutral, bare copper ground, black "hot," and red "hot" wire.

Wire Connectors

When installing nonmetallic wiring, distinguish the outside covering (the jacket) and the internal wires. The "wire" you perceive is the sheathing that covers the inner copper conductors. You'll find signs indicating the number and gauge of wires within the sheathing if you look closely. The sheathing color indicates the wire's function.

Black wires carry active electrical loads from the service panel to an outlet, lamp, or other location. Red cables are used to connect smoke detectors so that if one goes off, they all go off. They connect to a neutral bus bar which pulls and transfers power throughout the house. Despite their "neutral" label, they may nevertheless carry a charge if the current load is unbalanced.

Hot wires are white wires taped in black or red. The tape merely shows that the ordinarily neutral white wire is being used as a hot wire.

Green wires connect an outlet box's grounding terminal to an electrical panel's ground bus bar, allowing current to flow to the ground if a live wire contacts metal or another conductor. However, if the electrical system isn't operating correctly, green lines might still be active. Copper bare wire is the most common grounding wire.

Blue and yellow wires are seldom seen in NM cable but may be used as hot wires in an electrical conduit. The blue ones are travelers, which may be found in stairwell switches to regulate the same light.

DIY Wiring Tips

- To perform your wiring, you need expertise and tools.
- Have the required gear. Two examples are a voltage multimeter and a sheath or wire stripper.
- Learn the cables. To avoid electric shock and adequately wire your home, know which wires are which.

- Have more wire than you need. Make it three inches beyond the electrical box.
- Patch drywall using huge plates. Did you make a drywall hole too big? Replace it with a big electrical plate.
- Quality is not free. Quality switches and outlets are essential.
- Check the voltage before touching any wires or circuits. The multimeter will tell you whether they're safe to touch.
- Pay attention—instructions on YouTube.

Mistakes in Electrical Wiring

An electrical "oops" may result in short circuits, shocks, or fires. Here are some common mistakes not to make

- Electrical junction boxes should always be used to connect wires. If not, construct one and wire it inside.
- Remember the 3-inch minimum wire length. Don't cut your cords too short.
- Never leave sheathing exposed between frames, as in a ceiling. You should staple cable to the wall rafters or ceiling joists or in a metal conduit.
- Avoid using loose switches or outlets.
- Never install a three-slot receptacle without a ground wire.

- Recessed electrical boxes should not be concealed. Make a wall expansion instead.
- Clamp the cable to prevent wire insulation damage.

BASICS OF HOME ELECTRICAL INSTALLATION

Service and Meter

In most cases, the electric meter is linked to the service entrance pipe. It may also be connected to an electrical pole. It might come from above or below. The meter is a piece of equipment that measures monthly electricity use. Earlier meters had numbered dials, similar to a watch, whereas newer digital meters can be viewed directly from the utility company's headquarters.

Disconnect Switch

Disconnect switches stop current flow in electrical circuits. By halting the flow of electricity, disconnect switches allow emergency shutdowns, power switchovers, and maintenance. An enclosure, electrical connections, and an actuator make up a disconnect switch (handles, shafts, keys, etc.). The shell protects the links from external dangers while prohibiting user contact.

Electric Service Panel

The electric service panel links the street connections to the inner wiring of your house. The service panel connects the primary service wire (or service drop) from the outside to the exit wires that serve different house parts. These exit cables are called branch circuits or branch wire circuits.

HOW CIRCUIT BREAKERS WORK

The main circuit breaker panel is a big switch that secures your home's energy. The circuit breaker box also houses smaller sub-switches that connect to some regions of your home. Breakers are tiny switches that preserve electrical safety.

You'd only need to access the main circuit breaker panel for emergencies or maintenance as a homeowner. The utility company's electricity is transmitted via the meter to the main circuit breaker panel. The circuit breakers protect you and your family at risk of electric shocks, burns, and fires from your home appliances, HVAC system, or electronic devices.

The circuit breaker panel protects the wiring and prevents electrical shocks and fires caused by overloading or heat accumulation. The circuit breaker panel's safety mechanisms protect against incorrect grounding, short circuits, voltage fluctuations, poor wiring, and damaged insulation.

DIY Electrical Safety

Size is important: Always accurately measure the length of the wire you'll be working with, particularly if you'll be installing a new cable yourself. Incorrect gauging may cause overheating and, in the worst-case scenario, an electrical fire.

Amperage rating: Check whether all of your cables and equipment are rated for the correct amperage.

Use fuses sparingly: If a fuse blows, don't simply replace it with a comparable one. To begin, examine the whole circuit system for anything that might be triggering the trip. Second, make sure that your new fuse is an identical match to the original. One of the leading causes of electrical home fires is incorrect fuse size.

Know your watts: Always make sure you know what bulb wattage to use in your sockets. Using a bulb in a socket with a greater wattage than it was designed for may cause the bulb to overheat and perhaps explode or catch fire.

Don't overburden the circuit breaker panel: Use caution when changing connections to your circuit breaker panel. The maximum circuit capacity of the panel must never be exceeded. It all depends on how many amps a circuit is intended to handle.

Consult a pro: Consult a licensed plumber before putting wire close to plumbing or copper piping to verify that the wiring is safe from the piping.

Take precautions by

- Wearing protective clothes: Cotton long-sleeved protective clothing works well.
- Use safety goggles: To protect your eyes from stray sparks or sharp objects.
- Gloves made of rubber or leather: Check that your gloves have been tested and are appropriate for the operating voltage.
- Footwear made of rubber: When working with electrical wire, these shoes, also known as dielectric shoes, may help protect you from a lethal shock.

Don't Get Your Cables Mixed Up

When it comes to recognizing the right electrical device wiring, always start with the fundamentals. And, regardless of what expert electricians advise, always treat all wires as though they are live before disconnecting them from the circuit. This precaution provides additional safety while dealing with volatile systems with underlying flaws that are first invisible.

Resetting a Circuit Breaker

Most homes employ circuit breakers to shut off power when an overload or short occurs. Rather than turning off the whole house, the circuit breaker isolates the issue circuit. Avoid shock by wearing protective gear, drying your hands, and standing on a dry surface while resetting circuit breakers.

1. Disconnect all lights and appliances in the affected rooms.
2. Ensure the breaker box, surrounding area, and floor are dry (no water) before working with the components.
3. Open the circuit breaker panel using a flashlight. The circuit breakers have three positions - on, off, and center.
4. Find the circuit breaker in the middle or tripped position.
5. Flip the switch off, then back on.
6. Wait a few seconds to see whether the breaker stays on. If this happens, leave circuit breaker on and restore power. If the switch doesn't stay on, there's a severe wiring problem. Contact a certified electrician.
7. Assuming the electricity stays on, it's time to look into the problem. The most common causes are a shorted device or an overload of the circuit.

Check each light for short. If the breaker stays on, connect carefully. When the circuit breaker tripped when you plugged anything in, you've found the problem. Breaker reset after unplugging faulty the appliance. Look for melted insulation on the power cable to indicate a short. Smell or see charring on the plug and outlet.

HOW TO FIX A DEAD OUTLET AND RESET A GFCI

The challenge is determining whether the outlet is defective and must be replaced or functional but has another flaw. Determine the issue's scope first. Is it only one or several? Look at you. Are any lights out? Unplug devices from each GFCI outlet and check for a popped-out "reset" button. Be sure to check the breaker panel as well. Fuse boxes may exist in older homes with a non-replaced main electrical panel. Reset any tripped breakers. Find and fix any blown fuses. Turn on the devices and reconnect.

Knowing a room's wiring helps identify which outlets and switches are on the same circuit. Assume you work at home. The kitchen counter plugs are GFCIs, but not the computer table plugs. If the GFCI at the counter or the breaker trips, the non-GFCI outlets will be "dead" or without power. The table's non-GFCI outlet may work, but the upstream GFCI has tripped, and the power is out. That's why knowing a circuit's outlets and switches is critical. A non-GFCI outlet may activate a GFCI. Inspect the outlet using an electrical tester.

If just one GFCI has tripped, but the others seem to be operating, push the "reset" button until it clicks into place. If your finger doesn't fit, use a tool. Reconnect the device when it connects back in. Re-inspect the room to ensure the GFCI is working. If you've tried everything and still have issues, call an electrician.

WIRE REPAIR

The demand for electrical wiring is exceeded when outlets are overloaded with appliances, power strips, etc. The hot wire then burns or melts everything in its path, including the plastic outlet. This damage is a problem in older homes built back when life was not so dependent on electricity. Previously, the wire used was too thin to carry large amounts of electricity safely. If you notice electrical heat or a burning odor, turn off the power and call an electrician! You may be overloading a circuit.

REPLACING A FAULTY SOCKET

Follow these safety measures before beginning any form of electrical work:

- Turn off the main power supply at the consumer unit or fuse box. Remove the circuit fuse to isolate the circuit on which you want to work. Please keep this in your pocket to prevent misplacing it.
- Alternatively, turn off the breaker and lock it if possible, and leave a notice on the unit indicating that you're working on the circuit.
- Use a socket tester, voltage tester, or meter to ensure the circuit is not dead for lighting circuits.
- A socket may be damaged for various reasons, including a blow that breaks the faceplate or

overheating that causes burning. If the issue is burning, it is frequently the result of overloading the socket or loose connections in a plug. If you plug it back in without addressing the issue, the same thing will happen again.

Step 1: Disconnect the circuit. To double-check that it's dead, use a socket tester. Remove the socket faceplate by unscrewing it and pulling it away from the wall. Keep the old screws in case the replacements don't fit.

Step 2: Loosen the terminal screws and pull the cable cores free. If the insulation has been heating damaged, cut the cores back and remove the ends. If the earth core is bare, wrap it in green or yellow sleeving.

Step 3: Connect the red core(s) to the live terminal of the new faceplate, the black core to the neutral terminal, and the earth core to the earth terminal. Be sure all screws are tight. Reinstall the new faceplate. Use the original screws if the new screws do not fit the old box. To ensure that it is appropriately connected, use a socket tester.

Although you may increase the number of sockets in a room by changing single sockets to doubles, there may be occasions when you want an additional socket when none previously existed. In this instance, you'll need to install a ring circuit spur. This spur may be routed from an existing socket or a junction box linked to the cable run of a suitable ring circuit. RCD protection is required on the circuit.

REPAIRING A WOBBLY ELECTRICAL OUTLET

To repair a loose outlet, you'll need outlet shims, a wire tester, and a screwdriver. After you've gathered these tools, proceed with the following steps:

Step 1: Turn off the outlet's electricity. Your electric panel should have a circuit breaker that is designated for that room.

Step 2: Examine the outlet. Before proceeding, insert your wire tester and ensure that the power is turned off.

Step 3: Remove the outlet cover and screws.

Step 4: Remove the outlet from the box and hang it freely.

Step 5: Shim the outlets. Install outlet shims over the outlet screws. These shims will fill any gaps that may exist between the screws and the recessed box. Depending on how far back your box is, you may require more than one shim per screw.

Replacing and Testing

Tighten the screws and replace the outlet in the housing box. If it still seems to be loose, apply additional shims. Replace the outlet cover, reconnect the power, and enjoy your newly secure outlet.

HOW TO REPLACE A LIGHT GLOBE'S BURNED WIRE

Step 1: Remove the two 3 mm screws on the power adapter using a flathead screwdriver.

Step 2: Clean the power adapter's casing as thoroughly as feasible if necessary.

Step 3: Cut the wires to equal lengths using wire cutters.

Step 4: Carefully remove the wire cord using wire strippers to reveal 2 cm of wire.

Step 5: Re-insert the shell into the wire cable, past the exposed copper wires.

Step 6: Grasp the power adapter terminal and, if necessary, unscrew the terminal's 3 mm screws. Wrap one exposed copper wire around a loosened 3 mm screw and tighten it right away. The second bullet point should be repeated for the second copper wire.

Step 7: Insert the shell back into the terminal so that it protects the terminal. Re-screw the 3 mm screws that were removed in the first step into the shell.

Step 8: Insert the power adapter into a working power outlet. The light globe should now turn on successfully!

REPAIR A SQUEAKING BATHROOM FAN

Many loud bathroom exhaust fans may not need replacement. The vent housing is usually just full of dirt and dust. Dirt and dust build up over time, causing the vent to create loud or vibrating sounds.

1. Turn off the fan's electricity.
2. Remove the connection to the ceiling vent cover.
3. In the sink, clean the vent cover with hot water. Remove any dust and grime to allow good air movement.
4. Remove ALL debris and dust from the vent housing, fan blades, and blower wheel using a canister vacuum.
5. After you've cleaned off all debris and dust, re-test the vent by turning it back on.
6. If the noise has subsided and the bathroom exhaust fan is quieter, the issue has been resolved.

7. You need to adjust the fan or blower wheel after cleaning out the bathroom exhaust vent and fan or blower wheel.
8. Switch on the exhaust fan and use a flashlight to examine the fan blade or blower wheel to see where it is striking.
9. Once you've determined where the fan or blower wheel is striking, switch off the exhaust fan so you can adjust the fan blade or blower wheel.
10. Continue doing so until the fan blade or blower wheel no longer hits the housing.
11. If the fan blades or blower wheels are correctly rotating and no longer creating noise, apply a tiny drop of lubrication to the motor shaft, which may squeak and produce the noise.
12. Replace the clean vent cover after your bathroom exhaust fan is clear of dust and grime and no longer creating squeals or loud sounds.

When you turn on the exhaust fan switch, the fan should be as good as new and no longer make any noise.

REWIRING A LIGHT FIXTURE

Cut the electricity: Disconnect the wall plug. Never work with the power on.

Remove the lamp:

1. Remove the shade, unscrew the bulb, and pressure the socket shell at the switch to release the shell and cardboard insulator.
2. Do not use a screwdriver to disassemble the socket.
3. Extend the socket as far as the connected wire will allow. If you don't have enough wire, pull the cable up from the light's bottom.

Remove the plug:

1. Loosen the socket's terminal screws and pull the cable wires out. If the light is small and the cable is straight, remove the old wire and insert the new wire.
2. Never tug on an old cord if it resists.
3. Examine if the light can be dismantled for easier removal.

Unplug the power: Untangle a tangled cord by cutting it about 12 inches from the lamp's base, separating the two conductors, and stripping the ends. Rep with the other end of the cord. Twist bare new and old conductor ends together, then fold twists flat. Wrap the splice with electrical tape. Pull the old cable from the fixture's top while working the new line through. Cut the old cord when you have enough new cord.

Remove insulation:

1. If you use a new cable, split the end after passing it through the bulb.
2. Remove three to four inches of insulation from each conductor's end, then twist the strands together.
3. When removing insulation, avoid nicking the strands.

The terminal should be wired: Tighten terminal screws as needed. Each wire's twisted end should be coiled into a clockwise loop and inserted beneath a termination screw on the socket. The clockwise loop will tighten the wire under the screw head as each screw is tightened.

Trim any bare wire using diagonal cutters: None of the uninsulated wires may have exposed bare wire or loose strands. If bare wire is exposed beyond screw heads, unscrew terminals and reconnect.

Insulator connect: Slip the insulator over the socket shell, then the shell and insulator. Socket the shell into the cap.

Plug in: Attach a quick-clamp plug to the cable's other end. Insert the cable end into the plug's side slot and pull up on the top lever. The plug's metal prongs pierce the cord's insulation to make an electrical connection, exposing copper wires. If you use a screw-type plug, prepare the wire ends for socket screws and knot them. Wrap each wire around the prongs of the plug before tightening the bare end. Knots and loops prevent wires from accidentally touching and make cable removal more difficult.

Restore the lamp: Before putting in the lamp, tighten the wires under the screw heads and snip off any uninsulated conductors that hang over.

REPLACING A BROKEN PLUG

An Electrical Plug That Dangles From a Socket

The problem is with the receptacle if plugs often fall out. An outlet's receptacle is the two narrow slits where plugs go. Components of your outlet degrade with time. Used outlets and receptacles may arc, ignite, or create fires.

The easiest option is to replace a worn-out electrical receptacle. The peace of mind is worth the cost of new outlets.

When replacing an electrical box, rewiring an outlet is necessary. To avoid shorts, connect each wire to the right connection. If your electrical plugs keep falling out and you're not comfortable mending them, we recommend replacing them. An electrician can quickly fix an outlet to keep your home powered.

HOW TO REPLACE A HARD-WIRED SMOKE DETECTOR

First, cut off the detector's circuit at the main electrical panel. Remove the old detector from its mounting. Then, when disconnecting the three wires from the old smoke detector, remember: Wires are connected by red or yellow interconnecting circuit wires. Be sure to remove the previous mounting plate and any wire harness linked to your home wiring before disconnecting the wires from a plastic plug. Now connect the new wire harness to the three house circuits as illustrated. Then coil the metal wires together and secure them with electrical tape or wire caps.

On two-wire detectors, connect the black and white wires. Then install the new mounting plate and disconnect the new electrical harness. After attaching the new smoke detector plug to the wall or ceiling receptacle, put the backup batteries into the new smoke detector head. Reconnect the power and test the smoke detector.

SET UP A PROGRAMMABLE THERMOSTAT

Step 1: Remove the old thermostat

Shut off your heater and air conditioner. Remove the prior thermostat's cover. In some instances, you must unscrew the lid. Remove your old thermostat with caution, but leave the wires connected.

Step 2: Mark the wires for future use

Mark the existing wires. Attach a little masking tape to each wire and mark the wire's original thermostat connection with a letter. The letter generally matches the wire color, although not always.

Step 3: Unplug the thermostat

Wires should be taped to the wall or wrapped around a pencil or small screwdriver to prevent them from retreating into the wall hollow. Taking additional precautions now will save you a lot of unnecessary hassle.

Step 4: Verify the wiring and install the faceplate

Your current thermostat is not directly linked to a power source if it has just two wires. Batteries must power all programmable devices. If it has more than two wires, it's likely direct-wired, and replacement models will be more plentiful. Install the faceplate on the wall, then thread the wires through and connect to the new thermostat.

Step 5: Complete the thermostat installation and wiring

Match the cables' letters to the letters on the new thermostat as you connect them. Install the batteries, then click the thermostat to the faceplate, and finally snap on the thermostat cover. Re-turn the breaker to re-energize the furnace and air conditioner.

SETTING UP LOW-VOLTAGE OUTDOOR LIGHTS

Installing low-voltage lighting typically involves three steps: wiring, transformer installation, and connecting the lights.

Installing the Cable

Begin by setting the light fixtures on the ground. Fixtures should be 8-10 feet apart. Then, unroll the low-voltage wire spool and arrange it near the fixtures. Surmount impediments like a rock, tree, or fence using the cable.

Cut a two to three inch-deep hole using a square-bladed shovel. To dig a deep V-shaped trench, just pound the shovel into the ground and jerk the handle. Because the trench doesn't have to be perfectly straight, just walk around any pebbles or roots. No earth should be removed from the trench.

Set the cable into the trench and press it down with a 1/2-inch-thick piece of plywood. Using a shovel or other tool may accidentally cut the cord.

Install in the Lights

Low-voltage cable is constructed of two insulated stranded copper wires connected together. Peel them apart, leaving four inches between each wire, removing five-eighths inches of insulation from either side using wire strippers. Insert one wire under the A screw terminal and the other under the B screw terminal after passing them through the transformer's retention strap. Tighten the screws to secure the wires.

Install the Transformer

Next, anchor a 2x6 in the ground near an outside electrical outlet. Stainless or galvanized screws hold the transformer to the stake. It is secured to the stake using insulated cable staples.

An exterior electrical outlet needs a "while in use" plastic cover. The cover protects the outlet from rain and snow while enabling easy access.

Plug in the Transformer's Power Line

Next, wire each light fixture. Most landscape lighting is prewired with snap-on connectors. Just push the connector to the cable. The connectors' sharp prongs enter the cable and touch the wires. Replace the lightbulb if it doesn't work.

After connecting the connection

1. Elevate the lamp and stake it into the ground.
2. Avoid tripping over the hidden wire.
3. Check each fixture before continuing forward.
4. After installing all fixtures, fill in the narrow cable trench with earth and grass seed.

Rewiring your home may be a challenging task requiring a lot of expertise and understanding. If you plan to knock down walls, you may need to rewire your house. You must have a qualified electrician inspect your electrical system. You or an electrician will need to install new wires, outlets, and circuits to keep you and your family safe.

8

RENOVATING YOUR HOME'S PLUMBING

There are various distinct sorts of plumbing systems. Consider your bathrooms, toilets, showers, sinks, and maybe the dishwasher or garbage disposal. Each is in charge of a kind of water and gas intake or outflow.

PLUMBING 101: THE FUNDAMENTALS OF PLUMBING

Supply of Potable Water

The first form of plumbing is your potable water supply. This plumbing system supplies running water to the following appliances and plumbing fixtures

- sinks in the kitchen and bathrooms
- toilets, baths, and showers

- dishwasher
- laundry machine
- hose faucets for the outdoors

The source of water in the potable water system differs depending on where you reside. Potable water is most usually supplied by a regional water treatment plant that serves households and businesses. Water from wells is standard in more rural locations. In both circumstances, your potable water system is underground and linked to the water supply.

The main pipeline is a one half to one inch in diameter and links as it emerges from the earth to the main cutoff valve immediately before it enters your home's walls. Your potable water system is configured as follows.

Pipes

Freshwater is delivered to your house through underground connections. The main pipeline links to the cutoff valve and a network of pipes run throughout your home, under the floor, and behind the walls. When you turn on a faucet, potable water flows through these pipes.

Main Shut-off Valve

The main valve regulates your complete potable water supply and additional valves located throughout your house through individual fixtures. You or a professional will turn these valves off during installation, maintenance, or repairs.

Shut-off valves entirely stop water flow, allowing you to operate on pipes without flooding the surrounding environment.

Water Meter

Before your house gets freshwater, the pipes transport it via a water meter located outdoors near your property. Water providers check these meters regularly to determine your water use.

Water Heater

A pipe system links your main water supply to your water heater. Plumbing systems are divided into hot and cold lines.

Faucets

Water is controlled via knobs and faucets in your sinks, baths, and showers. The hot and cold knobs draw water from two separate lines, and the water comes out appropriately.

Understanding Your Drainage System

The drainage venting system contains the pipes that lead from the drains in your sinks, showers, trash disposal, and toilet flush system. This system of pipes and components collects wastewater from your house and transports it to a treatment facility.

Your drainage system is made up of the following parts.

Drainage Pipes

Pipes may be found in every fixture in your home that contains flowing water. As a result of their downward inclinations, these pipelines depend primarily on gravity to allow water to flow. Your home's wastewater drains to the main waste and vent stack, which links to an underground stack. The underground stack then connects to an underground sewage pipe, which leads to a city collection line.

Drainage Vents

Your home's roof vent includes a drain vent that allows air to enter the drain pipes. The airflow ensures that the effluent flows properly through the system. It is critical to keep this vent clear of debris to prevent a drain backup.

Types of Plumbing Pipes

Pipes are available in many varieties, some of which are ancient classics and others manufactured from contemporary materials. When deciding the sort of pipes to utilize in your home's plumbing system, you should evaluate each of these materials.

Copper Tubes

- Copper pipes can be used for indoor and outdoor plumbing.
- Copper pipes are not prone to leaking and may be expected to endure a long time.

Galvanized Steel

- It has a zinc covering, which causes corrosion and water discoloration.
- It often gets blocked and has low water pressure.
- Corrosion may cause lead to be discharged into your water supply.

Stainless Steel

- Although more costly than copper, it is more corrosion-resistant and durable.

Polyvinyl Chloride (PVP Pipes)

- PVC pipes do not corrode, rust, or deteriorate over time.
- Since they can handle high-pressured water, they are typically utilized to deliver the main water supply into your house.
- They are also widely used in sink drain lines and bathroom drain lines.

Chlorinated Polyvinyl Chloride Pipes

- It is more flexible than conventional PVC, and the pipes contain additional chlorine, making them safe for drinking water.

- CPVC can be used for hot and cold water, but they will shatter if they get frozen.

Pipes Made of Cross-Linked Polyethylene (PEX Pipes)

- Extremely adaptable: They may be used for hot and cold water supply, ideal for retrofits, and quickly snaked through walls.
- Although they have been certified for usage, many people are worried that the production procedure of PEX pipes may represent a hazard to the environment.

Grey Polybutylene Pipes

- They are simple to install and have a lengthy life expectancy.
- The disadvantage of this style of plumbing is that it is prone to leaks.

HOW TO REPAIR A RUNNING TOILET

The sound of a running toilet has irritated us all. Not to worry; the solution is most likely straightforward. A running toilet is frequently the result of a flapper or fill valve issue.

Start by checking the water level in your tank by removing the lid. The water level should climb to approximately an inch below the overflow tube's top. If the water level does not rise up the overflow tube, your toilet flapper may not be adequately sealed, allowing water to leak out of the tank and into the bowl.

Examine the flapper chain to see whether it is kinked or hung up on the lever, preventing the flapper from properly closing. If the chain hangs appropriately, with little slack, your toilet may have a malfunctioning flapper. The flapper must adequately seal the flush valve and should be free of rips and bumps.

Whether the water level climbs over the overflow tube, causing the toilet to run needlessly, check to see if the float cup is stuck or needs to be adjusted. Above the float cup, there should be a knob that controls the height of the float cup up and down, regulating how much water is permitted to enter the tank. If the float cup is not the issue, you will most likely need to replace the fill valve assembly.

Step 1: Replace the toilet flapper

Turn off your toilet's water supply. You should be able to detect a knob coming from the wall or the floor near the wall and below the toilet. Turn the knob clockwise.

Step 2: Take out the flapper

Drain the toilet tank by flushing it. Separate the lift chain from the flush lever and pull the flapper from the pegs on the overflow tube to remove it. With a bit of pull, the flapper should come off the pegs. Take the flapper to the hardware or home improvement store to ensure that you obtain a suitable replacement.

Step 3: Reinstall

Before replacing the flapper, clean the flapper seat to ensure the new flapper seals properly. Attach the new flapper to the overflow tube's pegs.

Step 4: Remove any slack from the flapper chain

When the flapper is closed, ensure there isn't too much slack in the chain connecting the flush lever to the flapper. Working the flush handle up and down ensures that the flapper completely opens. As needed, move the chain's attachment to the flush lever.

Step 5: Restart the water supply

Turn the water supply knob counterclockwise to reactivate the water supply to your toilet.

REPAIRING A LOOSE TOILET SEAT

Does your toilet seat wriggle around so much that it qualifies for a thrill ride? The first step is to find the two plastic bolts that secure the toilet seat to the bowl. They are generally located at the rear of the heart and are protected by plastic caps. Lift the covers with a tiny screwdriver to reveal the bolt heads.

Before fastening the bolts, place the toilet seat in the middle of the toilet. Tighten the bolts by turning them clockwise with your fingers or a wide tip screwdriver. If the bolts spin but do not tighten, use pliers to grab the nut on the bottom of the toilet while rotating the top of the bolt with a screwdriver. Tighten until the seat no longer wiggles.

HOW TO REPLACE A LEAKING FAUCET

A new faucet may improve the aesthetic of your fixtures while also eliminating any leaks, drips, or other issues you may have experienced with your previous tap. Make sure that the faucet unit you pick fully covers the mounting holes of the previous faucet. If you have a unique sink in your house, seek a faucet set that can adjust to match a variety of sinks. Once you've decided on a faucet model, follow these steps to install it correctly:

Step 1: Turn off the water supply and unscrew the tiny screw on top or at the rear of the faucet handle attached to the main body of the faucet. Some screws are concealed under a metal or plastic button or disc that pops out or is threaded. When you remove the button, you'll see a top-mounted handle screw. Use penetrating oil to assist in loosening it if required.

Step 2: Remove the handle and inspect the faucet assembly. Remove the packing nut using a big pair of slip-joint pliers or an adjustable wrench, taking care not to scar the metal.

Twist out the stem or spindle in the same manner that you would turn on the faucet.

Step 3: Remove the old faucet assembly from the sink and clean the sink around the faucet mounting location.

Step 4: Attach the spray hose if the new faucet has one. Then connect the hose to the supply stub on the faucet. The spray hose should be routed via its aperture in the faucet assembly, through its opening in the sink, and up through the sink's center opening.

Step 5: Insert the replacement faucet assembly into the sink's mounting holes. With the new faucet assembly in place, hand-tighten the washers and nuts on the assembly's mounting studs beneath the sink, ensuring that the assembly is in the appropriate position and any gaskets are correctly aligned. Then, using a basin wrench, tighten the bolts even further.

Step 6: Align and connect the old water supply lines to the flexible supply tubes with the new faucet. Check that the hot and cold water lines are connected to the correct supply tubes on the faucet assembly. When connecting lines, be sure you use two wrenches. One person holds the fitting while the other twists the nut on the water supply line.

Step 7: Turn on the fixture's hot and cold water supply. To clean supply lines and inspect fixtures for leaks, run hot and cold water at full speed. If there are signs of leaking, go through the process again to look for loose or faulty connections.

REPAIRING LEAKS IN PLUMBING JOINTS

A leak at a plumbing connection not only wastes water but also costs you. As pipe and fixture connections, threaded fittings are used, and if they are not correctly sealed, they can leak.

Here's how to repair leaky plumbing

1. Turn off the water supply.
2. Cut the pipe at least an inch away from the fitting on each side of the leak. This cut allows you to unscrew the fitting at the pipe's junction.
3. Now, using pliers or an adjustable wrench, detach the leaky joint. Hold one end firmly and move the other anticlockwise to loosen and separate the two parts.
4. Clean both male and female fittings using a wire brush to remove any old pipe corrosion, compound, or debris. A standard wire brush is ideal for cleaning the male fitting, while a wire bottlebrush is required for cleaning the female connection.
5. Apply a generous application of pipe joint compound to the threads on the male fitting; do not apply joint compound to the female side. Wrap the male threads

with multiple layers of tape if you're using thread tape instead of joint compound.
6. Connect the male fitting to the female fitting and tighten until secure, then use your pliers or wrench to add half turn.
7. Connect the pipes using a coupler. The ends of PVC pipes will need to be cleaned using a PVC cleaner. Connect the pipes with a substantial quantity of PVC adhesive and a connector. If you're using copper pipes, you'll need to sand the end of the pipe, apply pipe flux, and then link the two pipes using a copper coupler and solder them together.
8. To check for leaks, turn on the water supply.

HOW TO UNCLOG A BATHROOM SINK

The best way to unclog a clogged bathroom sink may be determined by what is obstructing it.

White Vinegar and Baking Soda

To unclog a drain, use baking soda and vinegar following these steps.

1. Remove the sink stopper and unscrew the drain lid.
2. You will need 1 cup of white vinegar and 1/2 cup of baking soda.
3. Pour 1/2 cup baking soda down the drain.
4. Pour the vinegar down the drain.

5. Allow the mixture to drain for several minutes or until the fizzing stops.
6. Pour hot water down the drain.
7. Repeat the technique three times more.

Plunge

These steps will assist you in using a plunger to unclog a bathroom sink.

1. Make use of a cup plunger.
2. Take out the stopper.
3. Tape or rag the sink overflow outlet shut.
4. Place towels or rags on the floor around the sink.
5. Fill the sink halfway with warm water.
6. Make an airtight seal over the drain using the plunger's cup.
7. Using fast, crisp motions, pump the plunger's seal up and down multiple times.
8. Check the drain to check whether the obstruction has been removed.
9. Repeat as many times as needed.

Remove the P-Trap

1. Wear rubber gloves and place a bucket beneath your p-trap.
2. As needed, loosen the slip nuts by hand or with pliers.

3. Hand-remove the p-trap and empty the water into the bucket.
4. Remove any debris or filth that has been trapped in the trap.
5. Using a bristle brush, clean the p-trap.
6. Reassemble the p-trap and test the drain.

REPLACING A SHUT-OFF VALVE

Step 1: Turn off the water supply to the area where you will change the valve.

Step 2: Buff clean the pipe on each side of the old valve using an emery cloth.

Step 3: Cut through the pipe on both sides of the old valve with a tiny hacksaw.

Step 4: Insert the new stop-and-waste valve between the freshly cut pipe ends.

Step 5: Using pliers, grasp the valve and tighten one of the valve's compression fittings onto one of the pipe ends using an adjustable wrench—a rep for the other end of the pipe.

Step 6: Reconnect the water supply, open and shut the new valve; inspect your work for leaks.

REPLACING YOUR DISHWASHER

Replacing an old dishwasher is a reasonably simple task, as long as you've adequately measured and your new dishwasher fits beneath your bench.

1. If it still works, try shutting off the water and running the old dishwasher for approximately 30 seconds to remove any remaining water in the bottom.
2. Turn off the water and unplug the power, water input, and drain hoses under the kitchen sink.
3. Put down a drop sheet or some cardboard to protect your flooring and be ready to clean up any spills from the now-disconnected pipes.
4. Remove any screws or bolts holding the dishwasher to your countertop or cabinets and gently push it onto the drop sheet or cardboard. To create room for the new unit, move the old one out of the way.
5. Examine the cupboards for any damage, then clean the floor under the old dishwasher.
6. Keep the cardboard to protect the floor while you wrestle the new dishwasher into position.
7. Check the new machine's handbook for any installation instructions or advice.
8. Adjust your dishwasher's feet so that it sits sturdy and level. When it's in position, you may need to

tweak it again, but getting it close now is more straightforward than when it's beneath your counter.
9. Power, water, and drainage lines should be fed through the opening in your cabinetry and connected beneath the sink.
10. When attaching the wastewater hose, make sure it's looped up and over in an arch. Keep the hose as high in the drainpipe as possible—if you don't, you risk creating a siphon effect in your drainage, which might harm your appliance. Then clamp the hose down and wrangle the new dishwasher into the space in your cabinets. Alternatively, before sliding it into place, tie everything to the floor with tape along the dishwasher's centerline so it doesn't tangle in the dishwasher's feet.
11. Once the dishwasher is in position, re-adjust its feet to ensure it is level and sturdy— this shouldn't take long since you have pre-adjusted them.
12. Turn everything on and conduct a test to ensure everything is connected and operating correctly, keeping an eye out for any leaks.
13. Anchor your dishwasher to the cabinets securely. When closed, dishwashers are relatively solid and confined, but they may topple forward when the drawer is pushed out to empty it if not correctly fastened. While every dishwasher is different, it's usually only a question of screwing in a few screws, so there's no need to ignore it.

Before beginning any plumbing job, no matter how modest, it's a good idea to acquire a feel of your plumbing system as a whole. Do some study and learn the fundamentals of plumbing, such as how a vent pipe works, how broad your drain lines should be, and how much pitch a waste pipe requires. The more knowledge you have, the less daunting things will be—and the more quickly you will be able to fix any difficulties.

9

FLOORING IT RIGHT

There are numerous factors to consider when renovating your flooring, and getting even one thing incorrect may cost you a lot of money. Colors, patterns, and the best flooring material for your house are all factors to consider. The first step is to assess the material's cost, durability, ease of maintenance, and even weather.

A BUYER'S GUIDE TO FLOORING

Laminate flooring is a popular synthetic wood or stone flooring material. Most laminate flooring includes a transparent protective layer over the pattern. Installing laminate flooring is cheap and easy. No particular skills are required to install laminate flooring; the pieces snap together easily and may be laid over any subfloor.

Wooden Flooring

Real solid wood flooring has been used as a flooring material for centuries. Hardwood floors are not cheap, but they add a lot of cosmetic and financial value to your home. Wood flooring may last decades despite its vulnerability to wetness. The wood may warp if you live in a rainy climate. Hardwood flooring is more costly, but it lasts longer and is less easily damaged.

Vinyl Flooring

Vinyl is a durable and low-cost artificial flooring option. Vinyl sheet is more durable, weather-resistant, and simpler to install than vinyl tiles. Many people confuse linoleum with vinyl. Linoleum, on the other hand, is 100% natural and possesses vinyl-like properties.

Stone Flooring

Stone flooring is one of the best flooring options since it lasts forever. Stone is a rigid, durable, and practically indestructible material. A stone floor may survive for decades after installation. Stone, like wood, adds value to your home. It is also a very eco-friendly flooring material. Stone flooring is an excellent option for hot summers. The stone is naturally chilly; it will keep your home cool even when the outside temperature is high.

Carpeting

Carpeting is by far the softest option. Carpets are less costly than stone or wood. They come in a rainbow of colors. They are also relatively easy to set up. Unfortunately, carpeted flooring is not very long-lasting and may need to be changed; every carpet is hard to clean and collects dust. So, if you're having a baby or have hyperactive kids, consider carpet flooring.

The sort of flooring you select will be determined by your budget as well as your needs. Vinyl or carpet flooring may be more appropriate for an apartment, but wood, engineered flooring, or stone is a more likely choice for a country home.

REFINISHING HARDWOOD FLOORS

If your hardwood floor has seen better days and you believe it may require a complete refinish, this is a task you can perform at home in the following steps.

1. Use a hardwood floor cleaner to clean the floor.

2. Remove any furniture and spray the floor with a hardwood flooring cleaner or your homemade vinegar-water mixture.

3. With a terry cloth mop or a towel wrapped around the mop head, wipe down the floor gently.

Preparing the Perimeter

4. Make sure you hand-sand the room and any crevices that the buffer can't reach with 180-grit sandpaper.

5. Working four to six inches out from the baseboard, rub the grain until the finish dulls and a powder appears. When refinishing hardwood, avoid using a sanding block since it may overlook variable regions in the floor.

Floor Finishing

6. Put your mask on and attach a maroon buffing pad to the buffer.

7. Move the buffer across the floor from side to side in the direction of the grain, overlapping each course by six inches.

8. The old finish turns into powder as you proceed, making it easier to tell which areas you've covered.

9. The buffer should be moving at all times, but it should be suctioned every five minutes or so.

Tack and Vacuum

10. Allow 10 to 15 minutes for the powder to settle in the room.

11. Replace the vacuum's filter and sweep the floor using a felt-bottomed attachment.

12. Sweep across the flooring strips to remove any powder that has collected between the boards.

13. Finally, use a microfiber cloth pressed with the grain to dry-tack the floor.

Cut Along the Edges

14. Put on booties over your shoes and wear an organic vapor canister respirator.

15. Pour some strained finish into a tiny plastic container after straining it through a cone filter into an unused sprinkler head.

16. Brush a three-inch-wide stripe alongside the baseboards at the furthest place from your door.

17. To prevent lap marks, you need to stop after 10 minutes if the edge of the stripe begins to dry.

Roll Out the Polyethylene

18. Pour out a one-inch-wide band of finish parallel to the grain—no more than you can spread in 10 minutes.

19. Finish the project with the grain and then across it, with a long-handled roller and a 14-inch nap cover.

20. To preserve a moist edge, overlap each pass and work fast.

21. Brush more finish around the edge after 10 minutes, then pour and roll for another 10 minutes. Continue until the floor is completely coated.

22. Wait 3 hours before repainting and a week before placing the furniture back in place.

HOW TO KEEP HARDWOOD FLOORS CLEAN

Many folks sweep their hardwood floors because it's what they've always done. Sweeping wood floors, on the other hand, only kicks dust into the air. That dust will ultimately settle back down, so you're only spreading dirt and allergies. Sweeping wood floors might thus be a waste of time and energy.

Using a microfiber dust mop or a vacuum cleaner is the finest way to clean hardwood floors. As an extra benefit, you will most likely only need to clean high-traffic areas such as foyers, living rooms, and corridors once a week.

The Best Hardwood Floor Vacuum

There isn't a single brand that you should rush out and buy as far as hardwood floor vacuums go. You should, however, keep the beater bar in mind.

The beater bar is the portion of the vacuum that is bristle-covered and rotates around. While this is useful for removing dust from carpet naps, it might harm the polyurethane layer on your hardwood floor. Fortunately, there are vacuum versions available that do not use beater bars. Some vacuums also allow you to disengage the bar not to spin while cleaning hardwood floors. If your vacuum does not have one of these capabilities, you can use an attachment designed specifically for vacuuming hardwood floors.

If you like cute techy devices, you can also employ a vacuuming robot to clean hardwood floors. However, skipping the mopping stage may be a good idea because these small electronic cleaning animals frequently use more liquid than hardwood can manage.

Take Two Extra Steps to Maintain Hardwood Floors

There are a few additional things you can do to keep your hardwood floors in good condition:

Purchase a Floor Mat

A mat placed inside the door might help catch debris before it reaches your hardwood floors. Your carpet should be long enough to allow for two to three steps before reaching the natural wood flooring for the greatest results.

Shoes Should Be Left at the Door

Place a shoe rack at the door or remove shoes in the mudroom. The dirt on the bottoms of your shoes will remain in the entryway if you leave them there.

That's all there is to clean hardwood floors regularly. It's a quick and simple operation that will keep your floors looking good for years.

HOW TO REPAIR SMALL SCRATCHES AND RIPS IN VINYL (PVC) FLOORING

Repairing scratches and cuts in vinyl flooring sheets or tiles is fast and simple. In all circumstances, the goal is to fill in the damaged region and keep the bottom layers of the soil from degrading.

You will need to thoroughly clean the affected area and remove any existing dirt or debris from the surface of your vinyl flooring.

Apply a specialized vinyl joint sealer or sealant to the scraped or cut portions of the vinyl flooring. Wax may also be utilized.

Fill with surplus material and then sand the surface till smooth. The general recommendation is to speak with specialists to choose which product to use in each circumstance and apply it. There are also kits available on the market to restore minor damage to vinyl flooring.

REPAIR BUBBLES IN VINYL (PVC) FLOORING

When water leaks or seeps, tiny bubbles may appear on vinyl flooring. Before doing any work, ensure that the surface is dried.

Then, from part to part of the bubble, create a horizontal slit with a cutter or a sharp blade, and push to allow the air inside. Since the surface will not be level, you will most likely need to put vinyl adhesive through the hole you created and apply pressure again.

To finish, throw a towel over the bubble and iron it. The idea is for the vinyl to rebond in the heat. If there is still a slight defect, you may remedy it as described in the preceding step.

HOW TO INSTALL WALL-TO-WALL CARPET

When you choose to install wall-to-wall, you can expect it to influence the room's appearance significantly. On the other hand, carpet may impact how a space feels, not only on your feet. Wall-to-wall carpeting acts as a natural insulator, preventing warm air from escaping while also absorbing sound. Furthermore, unlike hard flooring, it can prevent slips and cushion falls, which are crucial concerns if you live with rough-housing children or an older parent.

These are the steps

Step 1: Remove the old carpet and padding from the room; vacuum the subfloor clean.

Step 2: Nail down an additional tack strip beside the initial tack strips.

Step 3: Apply padding adhesive to the floor, along the walls, and at any seams.

Step 4: Place cushions on the flooring and fix seams using duct tape.

Step 5: Spread carpeting on the floor of the room.

Step 6: The carpet should be cut to fit around wall corners.

Step 7: When sewing two pieces of carpeting together, use a cushion-back cutter to trim the carpeting edges.

Step 8: Apply latex seam sealant to carpet edges and let dry.

Step 9: Align the seams between the carpeting pieces, then put some seam tape below.

Step 10: Use a seaming iron to activate the adhesive tape.

Step 11: Hook the carpet's edge onto the tack strips using a knee kicker.

Step 12: Using a stair chisel, force the carpet down onto the tack strip.

Step 13: With a double-bladed wall trimmer, remove any extra carpeting along the wall.

Step 14: Using a knee kicker and a stair chisel, press the rough-cut carpet edge into the area between the tack strip and the baseboard.

Step 15: Use a motorized stretcher to pull carpet taut across the floor; stretch carpeting toward each wall.

Step 16: Transition molding should be used to secure carpets at doors.

PAINTING A CONCRETE FLOOR

One of the most effective ways to create a visual impression in a space is to change the ground under your feet. If you're not ready to use your carpets and tiles, there's another option; painting your cement.

Prepping

To begin, you must clean and polish your concrete floor:

1. Use a concrete cleaner to remove carpet adhesive.

2. Degrease flooring with car-oil stains (such as in a garage) by scrubbing them with a metal brush and a solution of water and trisodium phosphate. It will begin to bubble—wait 20 minutes before rinsing it off. Degreasing will help the paint to cling to the surface.

3. Fill imperfections with cement filler.

4. Pole-sander the floor, then vacuum it in alternate directions until smooth.

5. Perform a moisture test. Tape a transparent piece of plastic into the concrete. Leave it for the night. In the morning, look for drops on the interior. Allow longer drying time if there is wetness.

6. Apply a masonry primer. Use self-priming floor paint to save time.

Painting

Choosing Your Paint:

7. When selecting paint, keep the location in mind. Water-based paints are the most economical and most suited to low-traffic areas inside, but oil-based paints are a little harder and better suited to patios and busier rooms. Choose epoxy, a resin that hardens rapidly and has a high sheen, for situations that need a firm floor. You can buy 100% epoxy paint, but it isn't easy to apply since it hardens quickly. There are water-based epoxies (which are generally used in houses since they are less stinky) and solvent-based epoxies. However, they include many chemicals.

8. Spill paint on the floor and roll it out in a 'W' shape for uniform distribution. You'll need a putty knife to smooth down any imperfections as you proceed.

9. Sand sections of paint that aren't adhering correctly. For the second coat, work over the difficult regions.

10. Apply a layer of concrete sealer to provide sheen and life to your floor.

DIY TILE INSTALLATION

Setting your tile may save you a lot of money and is a DIY project that everyone can do. While tile is gorgeous, it is also unforgiving; you cannot sand, caulk, or re-nail it. As a result, it's essential to have the task done the first time correctly.

In most remodeling situations, we utilize a floor leveler to flatten the floor rather than level it. Suppose your floor has deep pockets; mix up some floor leveler and pour it on. The trick is to find the proper viscosity; A touch denser than water, but not by much. It must be fluid enough to flow so that gravity may pull it into a low location. With a flat trowel, scrape off the edges.

Objects surrounding the tile move, but the tile itself does not. Basement flooring, walls, and countertops may all move. Red Gard is a waterproof crack isolation membrane. Red Gard is a 'bond-breaker,' akin to placing rosin paper beneath a wood floor. If the slab shifts, the RedGard flexes under the tile. It's also waterproof, which helps to keep moisture and humidity from groundwater at bay. It's also great for bathroom and wet surface improvements. Please apply with a paint roller and let it dry.

With a few exceptions, the beginning row of tiles should be the same width as the final row—regardless of the size of the room.

Keeping the tiles the same width becomes more difficult as the size of the room increases. And the more criteria there are, such as notches around room elements, the more you'll need to think about and prepare ahead. Cast a visible laser line, measure the remainder of the space, make minor modifications, and snap the final layout line in chalk.

Thinset should be around the thickness of peanut butter. When you comb it with a notched trowel, it should flow yet still hold up. The mud squishes behind the tile and attaches it to the floor. If you mix it too wet, you risk having to replace a tile in the completed installation. In addition, a paste-like consistency allows you to "back-butter" a tile. Back-buttering is the process of applying thinset to the back of the tile and the floor to compensate for a tile that is set too low in comparison to its neighbors.

Grout is the last step in any tile project. Changing the water often is a vital factor in ensuring that the grouting process goes well. Clean water is more effective in cleaning grout. Cloths that are damp but not soaked work best.

HOW TO REPAIR SQUEAKY STAIRS

To fix a noisy wooden stair, first, identify the source of the squeak. The squeak's location may also affect the repair. If a step squeaks from behind, it is likely detached from its riser. A squeak from either side suggests a loose step stringer. A riser is a vertical space between each step, while a stringer is a board that connects each riser. The saw-toothed stringer secures the stairwell.

Lubricate Joints

Your foot rests on the tread of the step. Cover the region between the riser and the tread below it with talcum powder, powdered graphite, or even baby powder to muffle a squeak on the back or side of the step. Using an oil-based lubricant may deform the wood or make the step slippery.

Pour the oil into the crack across the tread's back. Then, using your finger or an old paintbrush, thoroughly massage in the powder. The baby powder won't stop the tread and riser from moving, but it will minimize the friction that causes the squeak. If the noise reappears, put more powder to the crack.

Trimming Screws

If the front of the step squeaks, tighten the screws connecting the riser and tread. Trim head screws, which have a smaller head than regular screws and are easier to hide, are great for this.

Drill three pilot holes evenly spaced along the tread's front riser. To prevent foot harm, drill the screws into the tread with the heads below the surface.

To hide the screw heads, drill the screws deep enough into the board to prevent harming an unsuspecting barefoot. Pick a color that suits the wood on your stairs, although there are many alternatives.

Glue It

Nail the tread into the stringers on both sides of the staircase to remedy squeaks. Hand or pneumatically drive 2-inch finish nails at 45-degree angles apart.

Repeat on the same tread where the balustrade meets (the side away from the wall). Assemble the nails using something like a spring set. If desired, fill the indentations with a wood filler that matches the staircase's color.

REPLACE THE STAIR HANDRAIL

The handrail on your staircase may grow weak or loosened over time and may need to be replaced. If your railing covers the stairway entrance, you must ensure it is appropriately placed for safety reasons.

Do the following steps:

1. Place a 4-foot level on the first step and keep it plumb.
2. Mark the level where it intersects the top of the second step.
3. Calculate the height of the railing and mounting brackets, and note the bracket height on the level.

4. Mark the bracket height on the wall at the top and bottom of the staircase using a level.
5. Connect the two wall markers with a chalk line.
6. Mark the wall studs at the top, middle, and bottom using an electronic stud finder.
7. Drill 7/64-inch screw pilot holes on the chalk line and into the studs.
8. Attach the mounting brackets to the wall studs using screws.
9. Cut the handrail to the desired length, mitering the ends to 45 degrees.
10. Attach a mitered return to either end of the handrail using glue and nails.
11. The handrail should be primed and painted or stained and varnished.
12. Screw the handrail to the mounting brackets after it has dried.

You should purchase a tiny sample of the flooring before you make your final choice. Even though a piece appears beautiful in the showroom, you won't know how it will look in your space with your décor and lighting until you see it in person. Spending a few dollars on a sample ahead of time might save you hundreds or thousands of dollars on a flooring job you might not love.

10

WALLS AND CEILINGS

Here are some fast and straightforward methods to update the appearance of your house, whether you're getting ready to sell or want to give it a new lease of life. These low-cost home design ideas will help you remodel your house without breaking the bank if you're willing to put in a little time and work.

WALL TYPES AND FRAMING ELEMENTS

Before you start constructing a wall, you should be aware of the following essential factors.

- A bearing or structural wall bears the weight of the structure above it.

- A partition wall does little more than separate the internal area. It is not structurally necessary.
- The floor and ceiling framework elements are known as joists.
- A subfloor is fastened to the joists underfoot. Typically, the walls are attached to the flooring. Overhead, the drywall may be affixed to the underside of the ceiling joists, or a dropped ceiling grid can be fastened to them.

Painting Your Interior Walls

If wallpaper isn't your thing, you may paint the internal walls to give each space a new look. You may paint all four walls or make one a showcase wall by selecting a complementary color or a lighter or darker shade of the current paint.

Painting a space is simpler than most people believe. Preparation is the key to success. Filling and sanding any dents or defects will require some time and effort to create an excellent smooth base for the paint. Your local paint store can assist you in selecting the appropriate type of paint. Purchase high-quality paint; you'll find it much easier to use. There are numerous online videos available to assist you in painting your room like a pro.

Restore Worn-Out Floors

Due to their large surface area, floors tend to dominate the appearance of any room. Re-carpeting or re-varnishing worn-out floors can be a time-consuming task, but there are alternatives. You can quickly refresh your floors in less than a weekend with peel-and-stick tiles or a couple of coats of hard-wearing floor paint. Take measurements of your rooms and visit a significant hardware store for ideas and advice.

Replace the Backsplash

A new, clean, and stylish backsplash creates an eye-catching feature that draws attention away from less desirable aspects of your kitchen. Nowadays, you can have any color or image printed on the back of the toughened glass, including a mirror finish. However, if you're on a tight budget, self-adhesive tiles are a simple and inexpensive DIY option. The tile sheets are easily peeled and stuck in place. The only skill required is cutting a straight line with scissors or, in some cases, tin snips. If you're using peel and stick tiles near a stovetop, be sure they can resist the heat.

REPAIR HOLES IN THE WALL

Replacing Small Nail and Screw Holes

The smallest nail and screw holes are the simplest to repair. You can fill them with spackling or wall joint compound using a putty knife. Allow the area to dry before gently sanding it.

The steps are as follows

1. Before applying the patching compound, anything larger must be covered with a bridging material for strength.
2. Cover 1/2 inch to 1 and 1/2 inch diameter holes with a piece of adhesive-backed fiberglass mesh.
3. First, sand the area around the hole by hand to smooth out any rough spots. With a damp cloth, wipe away any sanding dust.
4. Then, cut a piece of fiberglass mesh to overlap the hole on all sides by at least 1 inch. Remove the paper backing from the mesh and press it against the wall.
5. Using a six-inch drywall knife, apply a coat of spackling compound to the repair.
6. Allow it to cure overnight, then carefully sand it before applying a second thin coat. After the second skim layer has dried, add a third skim coat if necessary.
7. Smear spackling compound through the mesh and over each hole with a 6-inch drywall knife. Allow the mixture to dry before gently sanding.

Replace Drywall Nails and Screws That Have Popped

One of the most typical reasons a screw or nail comes out of the wall is shrinkage in the timber underneath the drywall. When the wood used in the building has a high moisture content, it shrinks. Shrinkage may cause nail and screw pop at any time, but the home heating season can hasten the process.

Putting the Drywall Back Together

Screws or nails poking out of the wall indicate that the drywall in that location is not correctly attached to the frame. Simply screwing or nailing the fasteners back into the wall will not resolve the issue. To secure the drywall, install new screws in an undamaged place near the popped buckle.

Drywall screws are the most secure method of reattaching drywall to the frame. To secure ordinary 1/2-inch drywall, use one 1/4-inch drywall screw. Drywall nails are an additional alternative.

Insert a replacement drywall screw approximately one to two inches above the popped screw. Drive another screw underneath the popped one. Check that the screws are firmly fastened into the framework. You want the new screws to be slightly recessed without damaging the drywall covering. These screws restrict the drywall from shifting, preventing more popped nails or screws in the future. After you've secured the drywall with fresh screws, you may either reset the popped nail or screw or remove it entirely.

FINISH THE WALL

Fill up the hole using a lightweight spackling product for fast drying and high-quality results. Apply the compound to the wall using a drywall knife, dragging it over the surface to level it out. Remove the loose bits of drywall if the burst fastener caused it to shatter or crumble. A minor drywall repair completes the procedure, resulting in a smooth wall surface.

Repeat this filling procedure to cover the newly fitted screws. Allow the compound to dry in the area immediately around the screw heads. Reapply one or two more coats if required to cover the screws completely.

To get a smooth finish, sand the dry compound after the last application. To prevent removing vast pieces of the compound, use fine sandpaper. All you need to do is smooth out the area. The final stage in the restoration process is to repaint the room to conceal the drywall compound. To produce a smooth effect, blend the paint in with the surrounding area.

REPAIR A WATER-DAMAGED WALL

Water damage is the worst since it necessitates the repair of two items: whatever is leaking and whatever is damaged. Fixing the leak should be the top priority since it will continue to be an issue if it is not.

Step 1: Repair the leak

The leak is the greatest first step since it addresses the root source of the problem. Repairing the leak avoids the harm from worsening or recurring.

Step 2: Scrub the wall

If the wall is moist, mildewed, or moldy, use a weak combination of chlorine bleach and water to clean it. Allow it to dry after that—you can use a heater or blow dryer to speed up the process.

Step 3: Use a water-based primer and sealer.

Overall, the space will be better for painting. Allow it to dry before recoating it for a better seal. To prevent uneven regions, feather the edges. Feathering the edges will help prevent the wall from being water-damaged again and enable the paint to adhere to the wall better.

Step 4: Allow it to dry

It may be required to recoat the whole wall. Redoing the whole wall will need far more time and supplies, but the end product will be a flawless wall.

INSTALLING CROWN MOLDING

With foam crown molding, you won't only save money and have an easier time installing it, but it's also more pliable—enabling you to bend it around the curves of your home. It will be necessary to get a partner to help you complete your project, someone who can hold pieces while you attach the crown molding.

Measure the wall where the bottom of the crown molding will sit for each cut. Draw a thin line beyond your size to indicate the cut's direction and angle. Measure the wall where the bottom of the crown molding will sit for each amount.

Cut The Molding

The best way to cut inside and outside corner crown molding is to cut each piece upside down, with the ceiling side on the bottom and the wall side on top. Place the molding against the saw and draw a line with a pencil on the table.

Swivel the saw to a 45-degree angle to match the molding direction, align the board with the saw at the mark, and cut. The best way to cut inside and outside corner crown molding is to cut each piece upside down, with the ceiling side on the bottom and the wall side on top. Place the molding against the saw and draw a line with a pencil on the table.

Do not flip the boards upside down for scarf joints. The saw will flatten those joints. Instead, cut by tilting the saw blade to a 45-degree angle. During this cut, the swiveling section of the saw table remains centered. The boards should then fit together precisely.

Attach With a Nail

Put the pieces of molding into position on the wall using a nail gun. Fit scarf joints as closely as possible before nailing them in place.

Caulk

If the corners don't meet exactly, seal any gaps or spaces between the molding boards or where the molding meets the ceiling using paintable caulk. Fill the gap with a small amount of caulk and smooth it out with a moist towel. Repeat the procedure for visible nail holes as well. It's critical to obtain a tight fit on the outer corners since caulk won't assist you much here.

INSTALL WALL TILES FOR DÉCOR

Tile walls are sturdy and straightforward to maintain, in addition to their beauty and textural effect. With today's availability of marble, slate, ceramic, porcelain, and even prepared glass mosaics and wall tiles, creating a unique tile accent wall is simpler than ever. Here's how to do it correctly.

Step 1: Install the tile

Using a 14-inch notched trowel, comb latex-modified thinset mortar onto the wall. Since handmade tiles sometimes have uneven backs, apply a smooth layer of thinset on the backs of the tiles. Back buttering is an additional process that provides full adhesion between the surface and the tile.

Step 2: The grout should be bagged

The following day, use blue painter's tape to cover the edges of the art tiles, leaving just the grout line showing. Then, combine the grout and place it in a grout bag. Please close the open end of the bag and squeeze it with one hand to regulate the flow while guiding the nozzle with the other. Fill the joints surrounding the tiles.

Step 3: Smooth it using a tool

Pack the grout into the joint carefully using the edge of the grout float, or use a plastic teaspoon if you have one. Remove the tape and wipe up the grout residue with a sponge and water as usual. To prevent discoloration, treat unglazed or crackle-finish tiles with an impregnating sealer before grouting.

FILL IN A CEILING CRACK

Make careful to protect your workplace with a drop cloth. With the scraper, remove any old drywall tape or repairs.

Step 1: Install wooden support blocks in the attic above the crack. Then install drywall screws in the ceiling into the wooden blocks.

Step 2: Next, use the scrapper tool to cut a gouge in the ceiling to widen the fracture. The gouge will provide a surface to which the joint compound will cling.

Step 3: Tape the crack with a single strip of drywall tape. Then, apply the initial layer of the joint compound, pushing the mud through the taped mesh and into the break.

Step 4: Once the initial coat is applied, go over it with a moist double-sided sponge. Use the rough side to smooth out any lumps, then finish with the smooth side.

Step 5: Sand down the area if necessary, then prime and paint it.

Changing or adding artwork to a space is another easy and inexpensive approach to drastically transforming its appearance and feel. You don't have to spend a lot; choose a color and a theme, then go shopping at thrift stores, antique stores, and local markets. Making cardboard cut-outs the same size as your artwork and temporarily hanging them with blue tack is an excellent way to perfect the location. Alternatively, you may place your artwork on the floor in an area the same size as your wall. Canvas prints made from your vacation photos are another option to create unique décor for your house.

A DEFINITIVE GUIDE TO WALLPAPERS

Wallpaper has a longer lifespan than paint. To maintain the appearance of walls, they need to be painted every few years. Wallpaper can instantly transform a dull room into something beautiful if you need an instant fix. You can mimic wall finishes such as pressed metal, bricks, concrete, and wood at a fraction of the cost.

A GUIDE TO WALLPAPER TYPES

It's a good idea to acquire a sample of the wallpaper before making a considerable commitment and spending a lot of money. The sample will enable you to see if the color will look well in your space before you commit to buying it.

Roll

Wallpaper is most often purchased in rolls, whether for your home or workplace. Thus, cutting your wallpaper to the exact length for your space is easy and saves both waste and money.

Border

To inject some color and intrigue into your home, consider wallpapering only the border instead of the whole wall. Sizes for these borders vary from slimmer ones that fit in better to bigger, more ornate ones that stick out and grab attention.

Mural

Using murals is one of the quickest ways to cover a wall and give your house a unique appearance. Since murals tend to be huge, it's important to ensure the design and scale don't overwhelm your space before you acquire one. Murals may be found in a wide range of styles and colors to suit your home's interior decor.

Tiles

Tiles can be swiftly and fitted in almost any area, making them ideal for those who want to make a rapid change to their house but don't want to deal with the hassle of straightening out large strips of wallpaper. They usually peel and stick, so installation is quick, and you don't need wallpaper adhesive to use them.

HOW TO WORK WITH WALLPAPER: A FEW POINTERS

How to Pick the Best Wallcovering for Your Space

Wallpaper comes in a wide range of colors and designs. Vinyl is ideal for high-moisture areas like kitchens and bathrooms because of its water resistance. Non-woven papers and textiles are suitable for wet areas like bedrooms and halls.

Pick the Right Wallpaper Adhesive for the Job

Paper requires a different kind of glue, and understanding the difference between paper and vinyl is critical. Look for the correct label on your wallpaper.

Round-Up All of Your Dimensions

You'll have more paper to work with if you round your measurements. Plan on ordering at least two to four extra rolls of paper just in case there are any shortages. Whether you're a professional or not, you will make mistakes, and retailers may withdraw a particular design, so buying additional paper now will be appreciated later.

The Importance of Leveling Up

Even though your paper must be level, your home most likely isn't as well. You should always make sure that your initial sheet is exactly level before you start working with it.

When you come to a corner and things aren't flush, whip out the measuring tape.

Start With Smooth Walls

It's critical to begin with a smooth wall. After gentle sanding, wash your walls with a moist sponge and a mild detergent.

Have a Plan of Action

Draw Sew lines on the wall. If you don't, you risk having a pattern in the center of your wall that isn't quite right.

Razors Should Never Be Reused

Razors lose their sharpness quite rapidly, so don't be stingy with your usage of them. Avoid tears by making neat cuts. Buy a box of 100 to ensure you'll never run out.

Use Wallpaper Sweeps

When applying wallpaper, use a sweep rather than a brush. You can get one for a few bucks at any home improvement shop.

You Shouldn't Worry if You Notice Bubbles

As the wallpaper settles and the glue dries, air will most likely get trapped between the layers. This air is normal and will eventually disappear. If it doesn't, gently flatten the paper with the wallpaper brush after puncturing the bubble with a pin. Trapped air is normal and will eventually disappear.

HOW TO WALLPAPER LIKE AN EXPERT

Step 1: Make a plan for your layout

When learning how to install wallpaper, having a plan is crucial. To keep your pattern matching and looking straight, pay attention to the sequence in which the paper is stacked.

Step 2: Apply wallpaper paste

Roll up the wallpaper and remove it off the wall. Use a wall primer or sizer to paint the whole space. While you're at it, look for errors and smooth out the paper's curls by dragging it down the edge of your work table.

Make the paper four inches longer than the height of your walls and cut it into those long sheets. Repetition is vital while cutting since it helps keep pattern placement consistent.

Then, place a cut sheet face-down on the table for easy access. Then, using a paint roller, smear a thin layer of transparent premixed wallpaper paste over the paper's backside. Apply the paste to the paper's ends and edges by sliding it to the table's edge and sliding it back in place. Keep paste off the table so it doesn't stain the following page.

Step 3: Make a reservation for your paper

Reverse fold the glued back of the paper so that it meets in the center. Check to see that the side corners are entirely aligned. Try not to crease the folds while smoothing the paper over itself.

Set the paper aside to enable the paste to soak in and the paper to relax. Note the specific booking time indicated on the wallpaper label since this varies based on the wallpaper's subject matter.

Step 4: Align the first strip of tape

Begin at a room's back corner, next to a door. A parallel reference line needs to be drawn near the corner of the door if it is distant from the corner.

Hang the booking paper by its top fold on the wall. There should be about two inches of overlap at the ceiling and about 1/8 inch in the corner. Lightly push it in place.

Allow the book to hang by unrolling the bottom. Measure the distance between the text and the door casing. Make sure the paper is parallel to the door and still has at least 18-inch of overlap in the corner before adjusting it.

Step 5: Make sure you trim it properly

Use the edge of a paper smoother to tuck the paper into the corner at the ceiling. Work your way down, starting at the top and sweeping with the smoother after you've finished.

Use a six-inch tape knife to cut away any extra paper from the ceiling. Trim away any excess with a razor cut just above the blade. Work slowly. Cut and move the knife alternately.

Please do not use the razor and knife in the same motion. Continue to cover the door with paper until it is completely covered.

Step 6: Keep papering up your arms

Draw a plumb line on the adjacent wall -if there isn't a door or window. Put a piece of string in the nook. Overlap the current piece on the neighboring wall by 1/8 inch. Adjust the paper to maintain the same distance from the plumb line. The paper should be smooth. Trim the eaves and the corner of the room.

Hang the next strip of paper. Place the book's folded cover on the wall. A mere hair's width of space should separate the sheets when matching the design. Blow away any air bubbles by sweeping the paper smoother from the center to the perimeter of the picture. Use a sponge to remove any paste that has formed on the surface.

Step 7: Sew up all of the openings

Lightly push the top of the paper to the wall. Then softly rub the seam using a seam roller to smooth out the edges. Push the seam closed with your fingertip tips.

Unfold the bottom of the sheet and finish matching and sealing the seam. Then, moving from the edge three inches in, firmly roll the whole seam. As you smooth the paper, the seam will not open because of this.

Make sure the whole page is smooth. Step five shows how to finish papering the room by overlapping and clipping the corners. If the booked end of the strip begins to dry out before you hang it, wipe the wall with a moist sponge. When you hang the paper, the paste will be moistened again.

Step 8: Cut around moldings

At doors and windows, let the paper overhang the molding by at least an inch. Make a relief cut on the paper with the razor. From the molding's corner, carefully run the razor to the paper's edge. Follow the mold's instructions to the letter. Press the cut edge firmly in the connection between the molding and the wall.

With a tapering knife and razor, remove the extra paper flap. The whole sheet should be smoothed out. Wallpaper hanging mistakes are inevitable while learning the technique. Use a marker to paint the wall or the white border of the paper the same color as the form to hide tiny cutting mistakes. Some professionals may even color the edges of the paper may even be colored by some professionals so that seams are less visible as the paper shrinks as it dries.

Step 9: Put the switch cover on

Make electrical fixture cover plates invisible using paper. Make a swatch of wallpaper the same size as the plate and trim it to fit. The area surrounding the switch that matches the wallpaper should be cut off.

Place the plate face down on the paper after applying the paste to it. Turn the plate face down while holding the paper. Trim the corners of the plate to a distance of 1/8 inch. Then, attach the paper to the plate. Both papers should be held against the wall, and they should be adjusted to match the design on the wall.

Use a razor to cut out the holes for the switch or receptacle. Make Xs where the screw holes are located. Reinstall the wall plates using the screws provided.

THREE METHODS FOR REPAIRING DAMAGED WALLPAPER

Removing and Replacing Complete Wallpaper Panels

Removing and replacing the wallpaper may be the best option if the whole strip is damaged or unclean. Since non-woven wallpapers can be easily removed, they are ideal for changing entire rolls of wallpaper. However, you should proceed with care to avoid damaging the neighboring areas. Contiguous strips are more vulnerable to damage when removing paper-based, vinyl, or other wallpaper materials that must be scored and soaked before removal.

You should pay particular attention to pattern alignment while cutting a fresh strip of wallpaper. If the wallpaper adhesive is applied directly to the wall, extra attention should be paid to the seams on the adjacent strips while using it. Undamaged strips should have any damp adhesive residue removed as soon as possible.

How to Fix a Wallpaper Blister

Cutting and aligning the pattern is all that's required to construct a patch. If you're using tacks or masking tape, apply the patch to the wall. Use a utility knife and a straight-edge to cut through the patch and the wallpaper. Set the patch aside and use a moist sponge to soak the wallpaper. It ought to be easy to remove.

Make sure the new wallpaper matches the original in terms of pattern. Apply a tiny amount of glue to the patch's back before sticking it to the wall in the manner seen on the right. Smooth it out with a steam roller and secure it securely in place. Wipe off any glue that gets on the adjacent wallpaper as quickly as possible. Allow enough time for the wall to dry after cleaning.

How to Remove and Repair Wallpaper Bubbles

If you see bubbles, this might be an indicator that there is moisture in the wall. To fix a blown bubble:

1. Use a clean, wet towel to moisten the affected area.
2. Slit the bubble using a utility knife or razor blade.
3. Make a V-shaped slit or one that follows the pattern of the wallpaper rather than a straight cut since this will hide the cut and make gluing simpler.

4. Push glue through the incision using a thin putty knife.
5. Use a sponge dipped in water to distribute the adhesive under the bubble entirely.
6. Smooth the wallpaper to the wall and wrap it up.

If you know how to wallpaper, it's an easy method to decorate your home with various patterns, colors, and textures. You can wallpaper a room's four walls or use feature walls to your advantage. Whether you want a cool alcove or a pattern-filled maximalist lounge, there are a plethora of wallpaper options at your disposal.

THE A-Z OF PAINTING

Beginning DIY'ers and new homeowners must know how to paint a space effectively. After all, it's generally painless, affordable, and simple to remedy if anything goes badly wrong. But before you take your roller and start rolling on your first coat, make sure you have a strategy in place.

PAINTING BASICS TO KNOW ABOUT

Preparing the Walls for Painting

Whether you want to finish with wallpaper or paint, preparing the walls for plastering is crucial to receive the most satisfactory results. To get the prep portion correct, follow these six steps:

1. Make sure there is no wallpaper on the wall.
2. Clean the walls to get rid of any undesirable oil and filth.
3. Examine your walls for cracked or peeling plaster, then scrape these places to remove them.
4. Apply scrim tape (a tiny mesh that clings to the wall) to any gaps after you've scraped the walls clean. This tape will keep the fissures from showing through your new paint layer.
5. As a primer for the wall, use PVA glue or blue grit.
6. If you're unsure, get help from an experienced plasterer who will know the optimal conditions for painting your walls.

You'll need to invest in the correct paint to cover over dark colors with light colors. You can emulsion a wall, but you'll need a lot of coats to get a solid covering. And having more coats implies having more time. Any primer should ideally be white since this gives the greatest foundation coat for your light color of choice.

Prepare your walls by filling any gaps and sanding them after they're dry. At the same time, use fine sandpaper to run over the walls to promote primer adherence swiftly. If necessary, scrub with sugar soap.

Rollers and Paint Brushes

Painting moldings and window casings with foam brushes is a delicate task. These brushes are only suitable for one usage since they're difficult to clean and prone to tearing.

Acrylic paints, as well as water-based and latex paints, are applied using synthetic bristle brushes. Make sure a manufactured bristle brush has a broad head with uniformly scattered bristles before buying it. Brushes with a lower price tag may have gaps in the center of the head.

Straight or split-ended bristles are offered on polyester synthetic brushes. Split ends provide superior coverage, requiring fewer strokes to paint a surface. Latex paints are applied using these brushes.

Animal hair is used to make natural-bristle brushes, which are primarily used with oil-based paintings. The bristles will dry out if you use latex or water-based paints.

When used with latex paint, foam rollers produce an equivalent finish to a paint sprayer. Foam rollers may also be purchased in the form of a wheel, allowing the user to maneuver more easily around bends.

Type of Paint

Water-Based

If you've previously painted your surface with an oil-based solution, be careful about converting it to water-based paint since it may not adhere as well.

- Water-based paints have the advantage of being fast to dry and may be used on practically any surface.
- It maintains its color over time and does not yellow or fade in direct sunshine.
- Water-based paints have a few drawbacks: they aren't as vibrant as oil or urethane-based paints and don't last as long.

Oil-Based

Oil-based paint is recognized for its excellent durability and rich gloss, and it may be used on practically any surface. However, oil paint creates potent fumes that may be oppressive, and it cannot be wiped away with water.

Oil-based paints provide the following benefits

- ideal for high-moisture spaces like the bathroom
- firm, lasting finish

Oil-based paints have several drawbacks

- It is difficult to clean.
- VOCs may be dangerous to inhale.

Finishes of Paint

Sheen choices differ per manufacturer, but they all have a few things in common. As the endurance of modern paints increases across all sheen levels, many individuals are experimenting with new methods to mix and match them.

Matte paint is the slightest reflecting sheen possible, with a velvety texture that helps cover flaws in walls and ceilings while also providing tremendous color depth. It is often regarded as the standard sheen for walls.

Eggshell and satin paints contain some reflectivity and are widely used in demanding situations, such as kitchens and bathrooms, where simple washing is sought without a glossy finish.

The most reflecting sheens are semi-gloss and gloss paints, perfect for kitchens, doors, window trim, accent walls, and bathrooms. Their durability and easy maintenance enable repeated cleanings. They are often seen on baseboards, moldings, and doors.

It's crucial to remember that the quality of the paint you chose is only as excellent as the tools you use to apply it. Although you may believe that saving money by utilizing rollers or brushes is a brilliant idea, employing high-quality equipment can help you obtain the greatest results.

HOW TO PAINT A WALL

Always Start With a Plan

You'll need a strategy before you even take up a paintbrush. Is it also time to spruce up the ceiling? How about the edging? Take into account your selections for the walls as well. Will you choose a single color, or do you wish to experiment with two colors (maybe on an accent wall)?

Choose the Ideal Color

Colors seem brighter on the wall, and the light in your space may dramatically alter how the color appears. It's an excellent issue to have; although you'll eventually discover what you're searching for, deciding on the appropriate color might be a lengthy process. After selecting a few contenders, purchase sample cans.

Make a Swatch of Paint

Paint swatches on the wall after you have sample cans in hand. Try two coats of color on a 12-by-12-inch square to get a good sense of how the color will appear in your area. It's a good idea to place swatches in sunny and shaded locations if your space has both since this might impact the final effect.

You could also apply two coats of paint on a foam board and stick it to the wall. This foam board is a good alternative for individuals who don't want to start painting right away since they won't have to deal with odd color streaks on their walls. For this sort of sample paint, use a low-cost foam brush. You won't squander money or dirty a lot of brushes this way.

Calculate the Amount of Paint You'll Need

Many stores provide helpful calculators you may use to figure out how much paint you need. Always double-check the container, but a gallon should cover around 250 to 400 square feet. For touch-ups and errors, you'll need a bit more.

Collect the Necessary Supplies

Though the surface and size of what you're painting will have a direct impact on the specific list of materials you'll need, it's a good idea to have a mix of the following things in your toolkit

- tape
- tarps
- brushes for painting
- roller for painting
- tray for painting
- stirring stick
- paint

It is also useful to have an extension pole so you can put the ladder away after the edging stage, a paint can opener, and a pour spout to keep the mess to a minimum.

Prepare the Area to Be Painted

First, clean the walls from floor to ceiling with a dry sponge or cloth, and scrub any extra-grimy areas with a damp sponge or cloth; paint won't stick as well to a filthy surface that has dust or cobwebs. Allow drying completely before painting.

Avoid paint splatters and spills on the floor and any furniture you can't relocate. Fabric drop cloths are preferable to plastic ones for the floor since plastic might be slippery beneath your feet or worse, the ladder.,

Remove outlet and light switch plates, then use painter's masking tape to tape off any sections you don't want painting—moldings, baseboards, and window frames.

Prime Your Walls

When you're attempting to paint a room in one day, this may be a bit of a stumbling block. Painting a light color over a dark wall needs a priming coat, two coats of paint, and at least six hours of drying time.

Mix and Get Started

Even if the retailer shakes the paint for you, a good stir will guarantee that the color is well mixed. Start with the lighter color if you're painting a room with two colors, such as stripes. Run painter's tape over the divider once it's dry, then paint the darker color.

Here's how you paint a room one color using a roller and a brush

- To "cut in," use an angled brush or a sponge tool to paint a two-inch swath around the margins of the woodwork and the ceiling, or use an angled brush or a sponge tool to paint a two-inch swath around the borders of the woodwork and the ceiling.
- Use a 1/4-inch nap for smooth surfaces, a 3/8-inch nap for semi-smooth surfaces, and a 5/8-inch nap for rough surfaces; if you use the incorrect tool, you'll end up with too much or too little paint.
- Get a paint tray and roller ready. If you're using latex paint, Rothman recommends wetting the roller first.
- Fill the paint tray's well, roughly a quarter full. Then, when you're ready to apply the paint, roll the roller back and forth in the well until it's evenly coated. Finally, on the top area, rotate the roller back and forth to remove any excess.
- Using the roller, fill up the unpainted center area. For the equal paint dispersal, use overlapping 'W' or 'M'-shaped strokes.
- Let the first coat dry before applying a second layer. Use plastic wrap to cover the tray and brush, contact the paint surface between applications, and refrigerate.
- Keep a wet cloth on, ready to clean off any new

splatters. With a credit card or a plastic spatula, scrape off any dried drops.

Time to Tidy Up

1. Using a faucet, rinse your paintbrush and roller until the water runs clear.
2. Return the excess paint from the tray to the can and close it securely with a paper towel over the lid and a hammer on the lid edges. Rinse the tray well.
3. To avoid the bristles from spreading out, re-wrap the brush in its original paper wrapper after they're dried. Wrap a thick piece of paper around the bristles and fasten with tape.
4. Before you call it a night, remove the masking tape at a 45-degree angle to prevent damaging the finish.

PAINTING YOUR CEILING

Ceilings are sometimes neglected, but with bright color and a faultless finish, you'll encourage people to glance up and appreciate your good work.

Instructions

All successful initiatives begin with thorough planning. So clear the space, put down a drop sheet, and gather your ladder, brush, tape, roller, extension pole, and tray.

Step 1: Start by scrubbing your ceiling. With a clean brush, remove cobwebs and wash the area. Skipping this process might result in problems down the road.

Step 2: Tape the cornices, edges, and any downlights with tape.

Step 3: Begin by cutting in where the roller won't reach, just like you would with a vertical wall. To make a border, paint around the downlights and borders using a brush.

Step 4: Begin in one corner and proceed smoothly in a parallel motion after you've equally loaded your roller. Roll as far as you can into the previously brushed parts. Work in one-meter chunks, painting across and then down for the greatest effects.

Step 5: You may start laying off the paint now that you've done a significant area of your ceiling and it's still moist. This laying off is an essential step in creating a consistent and smooth finish. Begin at the top left corner of your ceiling with an unloaded roller and softly draw in a straight line towards you with no pressure. Repeat this motion, slightly overlapping your previous movement so that your roller scrapes away the line left by the preceding stroke. New brush strokes will not develop if you use a mild touch.

Step 6: If your ceiling needs two coats, wait two hours for the first coat to dry before re-cutting your top at step four. Clean up using environmentally friendly paint disposal procedures and admire your lovely new walls.

SPRAY PAINTING WALLS AND CEILINGS

While using a paint sprayer may seem a speedier application technique, this is not always the case. When choosing a tool for your paint job, consider the surface, its location, and how much time you have. Examine the advantages and disadvantages of spraying vs. rolling paint to determine which equipment and method are ideal for your job.

Which Is Easier?

Spray Painting Isn't as Simple as It Seems

If you've never used a paint sprayer before, don't expect it to be as simple as it seems. It takes a lot of trial and error to get an equal application with a paint sprayer. Drips runs, uneven coverage, and paint all over the place are common problems for beginners. But it doesn't mean you can't accomplish it. Sprayers are available in a variety of cheap, easy-to-use types that are ideal for practice. If you have some paint on hand and want to put your spraying talents to the test, go ahead and try it.

Rolling Paint May Be Equally as Quick as Spraying.

Most DIYers prefer spraying over rolling paint because they believe it will take less time to complete the job. That isn't always the case. When you use a sprayer, you'll spend more time assembling your equipment, meticulously masking the area, and cleaning up than you will spray. Since the prep work for spray painting takes much longer than rolling paint, the overall project time is nearly the same.

Stopping your project and resuming another day isn't a massive issue if you're distracted or tired of rolling—you can wash your roller or place your paint-covered equipment in a zip-lock bag to keep them fresh until you restart. However, once you've loaded a sprayer with paint, you're committed to using it until it's empty since paint left in the hose or gun of the sprayer will dry and produce blockages.

13

HVAC MAINTENANCE

Insulate your house to keep it warm in the winter and cool in the summer. By decreasing cold breezes and heat losses via the walls and roof, it increases thermal comfort. You'll have a more consistent temperature throughout the year, making it a more comfortable place to live.

UNDERSTANDING HOUSE INSULATION

Fiberglass: a kind of insulation made out of very tiny glass fibers found in most houses. It's usually found in two forms of insulation: batts and rolls and loose-fill insulation. Unfinished walls, floors, and ceilings may all be covered with fiberglass.

Rockwool: a form of insulation consisting of natural rocks and minerals. Stone wool insulation, mineral wool insulation, and slag wool insulation are other names for it. Rockwool's remarkable ability to filter sound and heat allows it to be used in a wide variety of goods.

Loose-fill: small bits of fiber, foam, or other elements make up loose-fill insulation. These microscopic particles combine to produce an insulating substance that can fit into any gap without causing damage to the structure or finish.

Rigid foam: an innovative building and construction material that can lower a building's energy usage while also regulating interior temperature. An adequately placed rigid foam board provides a layer of moisture protection.

Spray foam: is an excellent insulator and vapor barrier, but it contains chemicals and must be handled with caution. While DIY kits are available at hardware and large box retailers, experts urge that customers employ professionals to conduct the task.

HOW TO KEEP YOUR HOME WARM IN THE WINTER

Replace your Storm Door's Screen

When autumn arrives, it may be time to consider replacing your storm door's screen with a solid glass pane. Even though you'll be closing your main entrance for the whole winter, the additional layer of protection on the storm door will be invaluable in avoiding drafts and keeping the cold out.

Seal Drafty Doors

Fill gaps between the sides and bottom of your door and the door frame with rubber weatherstripping. Use a double draft stopper if the gap between the bottom of the door and the floor is large. This stopper consists of two cylindrical pieces of foam that slip onto the front and rear of your door to keep drafts out from below the door.

Ensure That Your Water Heater Is Properly Insulated

You can keep your water warmer during the winter months by placing a "jacket" on your water heater and without having to spend as much electricity on heating it. To protect your water heater, get a fiberglass jacket from a home improvement shop and wrap it over it like a blanket. Adding this additional insulation layer will substantially minimize heat loss and repay the money you invest due to the money you will save.

Use Thick Curtains

Curtains are lovely, light, flowing, and ideal for summer, but winter needs a different look. If your home's windows are particularly drafty, it's a good idea to invest in some long, thick, and heavy drapes. Hanging these thicker curtains will make a significant difference in keeping out the cold and in the heat.

ADDING A HUMIDIFIER TO YOUR FURNACE

Making a Mark and Cutting a Hole

Use a template and a marker to mark a hole where you will install the home humidifier. The outline is drilled at the corners first, and then the hole is cut out using aircraft snips. The mounting plate must be in place before drilling the screwed hole, and then it is fastened to a mounting plate using sheet metal screws.

The humidistat is generally installed to return cold air at least one foot above the humidifier. After cutting out the hole, connect the low voltage and fasten the thermostat with the tin screws that come with it.

Install the Electrical for the Humidifier

Connect the humidistat to the furnace control according to the manufacturer's instructions. If you haven't completed the wiring and your equipment uses a step-down transformer to convert 120 volts to 24 volts, turn off the power. The humidistat may then be wired and the transformer installed. The diagram below illustrates how to do it.

Connect the Humidifier Bypass For The Furnace

Connect the humidistat to the solenoid valve using the right size nut, attach the nuts and wire ends, and tighten the nuts.

Connect the Humidifier to the Water Line

If local regulations allow for direct tapping of a water line, install a saddle valve on the waterline. The saddle valve won't be able to cut off the water line and install the at-fitting. Then run a line to the humidifier, followed by the compression fitting to make it quick. Then you may install a bypass line in the HVAC system to produce water vapor.

CONSIDERATIONS FOR THE FURNACE

When your furnace breaks down and you can't get through the winter, it's time to call in a professional heating company to assist you in getting through the season. It's usually a good idea to get your furnace inspected before the winter months begin, so you're not caught off guard when you want to use your heating and it breaks down.

ADJUSTING YOUR THERMOSTAT

The mechanical contacts of a thermostat will need to be cleaned from time to time to preserve accuracy. Remove the thermostat cover with caution first. Then, using a soft cloth or a Q-tip, remove any dust or grime you detect. Remove any surface corrosion using an electrical contact cleaner if you see it. If cleaning your thermostat doesn't solve the issue, you might try the following adjustments:

Adjust the Heat Anticipator

Adjust the heat anticipator if your furnace turns on and off too often. Look for a little lever underneath a scale with a longer arrow. Moving the level in that direction may lengthen the cycle time of your HVAC system. However, keep in mind that lengthier cycle periods will be less successful at maintaining the appropriate temperature in your house.

Performing a level check: Some thermostats contain a mercury vial which must be leveled to ensure correct temperature regulation. Use a carpenter's level to validate this. Adjust the thermostat's positioning till it's straight if the measurement is off.

Calibration screw adjustment: Screw-type thermostats have a tiny screw on a coil that you may adjust for precision. Different calibration processes apply to additional items, so check your handbook before proceeding.

If you're still having issues with your thermostat or don't want to make the modifications above yourself, contact a skilled HVAC technician for help. It would be best if you didn't put off dealing with thermostat issues for too long. The better your thermostat functions, the more dependable and cost-effective your HVAC system will be.

EXAMINE AND REPLACE YOUR CLOGGED FILTER

Replacing your furnace filter is a fast and easy activity that protects your HVAC components while increasing your indoor air quality.

By holding it up to the light, you can detect whether it's time to replace it. If no light passes through, replace the filter. Another clue that your furnace filter needs to be changed is a dusty, unclean odor coming from the vents when the blower is turned on.

Make sure your furnace is switched off before replacing the filter. There should be no air coming out. Make sure your filter points are pointing in the right direction. Filters are designed to catch particles thrown in one direction. It's possible that installing your filter backward may limit its efficacy.

Cleaning the material that accumulates on your filters can improve airflow. Your air handler has to work harder to compensate for the blocked airflow when your air filter is clogged. Reduced air movement through your heating and cooling system might cause your heat exchanger to overheat and shut off too rapidly, which can raise your power cost.

INSTALLING A BATHROOM FAN

A bathroom fan installation is not a chore for the faint of heart since it entails removing drywall, maybe drilling through joists, and almost likely blasting through an external wall or roof. You may hire an HVAC contractor for $150 to $700. Here are some options you'll have to make if you decide to install a fan yourself:

1. Place a modest fan in your separate bath if you have one. Place the fan between the toilet and the tub or shower if your toilet is part of the bathroom.
2. Exhaust is vented via the fan's associated venting and out an outside wall or roof. Venting odorous, moist air into an attic or crawl space can damage rafters and encourage mold development.
3. The goal is to take the shortest, straightest route possible from the restroom to the outdoors. Every additional foot and curve in the venting creates more friction, lowering air draw and fan efficiency.
4. Appropriate ventilation travels up into your attic, then along or through floor joists to the eaves. Then vent it via a soffit. In other cases, running the vent straight out a wall or via a vent stack in your roof may be more feasible.
5. Make sure your bathroom door has at least 3/4-inch clearance from the floor during installation so that "makeup air" can readily replace the sucked-out air, placing less strain on the fan.

MAINTENANCE METHODS FOR AIR CONDITIONERS

Since parts of your air conditioning equipment are located outside and within your house, you should spend time on both.

Maintenance of Outdoor Air Conditioning

Although your condenser unit may look scary, keeping it clean and working is relatively simple.

Remove Any Debris

There should be as little trash in the unit as possible. Removing the cap and cleaning the interior of the condenser with a shop vac is a beautiful method to get rid of any leaves, tree branches, gravel, or muck that has accumulated.

Inspect the Insulation on the Coolant Pipes

Place a substantial insulation layer over the line that transports the refrigerant through your air conditioning system. These protective linings may be damaged by exposure to the sun. Check on this insulation frequently since it keeps the refrigerant cool and protects the pipe from damage.

Maintenance of Indoor Air Conditioning

Make Sure Your Filter Is Working Efficiently

To keep dirt and grime out of your blower, you'll need a good filter. Every three months or so, replace the filter. A new filter helps your air conditioner to run more efficiently and prevents performance problems.

Look For Any Leaks

Unfortunately, not all air conditioning maintenance is do-it-yourself. If you notice a leak in any of your AC unit's refrigerant lines, you should seek expert assistance.

14

CARPENTRY & WOODWORKING

Woodworking encompasses many crafts and thousands of years of experience, from creating chairs to cupboards. There's a lot to discover and learn about various woods, proper ways to work with them, and endless design possibilities.

EQUIP YOURSELF WITH MUST-KNOW BASICS

Read this comprehensive guide to woodworking methods and suggestions before you begin.

Safety Rules

If not utilized appropriately, woodworking tools may be harmful.

- Only utilize woodworking machines that you have been adequately and carefully taught to operate.
- Carefully read the owner's handbook.
- Before using any tool or equipment, be sure you read the instructions. If you have any concerns about doing the task safely, ask questions.
- When working with a saw or fine particles, always use safety glasses or goggles and a respirator.

Avoid these Blunders

- Wearing loose clothes, work gloves, neckties, rings, bracelets, or other jewelry that might get caught in moving components.
- To prevent harm from kick-back, do not stand directly behind stock that is being cut, planned, or joined.
- While operating a machine, do not remove sawdust or clippings from the cutting head by hand.
- Do not leave unattended tools running.

Must-Have Tools

- saws with a high torque
- planes
- hand saws
- sanders
- files

- hammer
- square sawhorses
- workbench
- mallet
- drill
- screw gun
- tape measure
- clamps

CHOOSING LUMBER

When looking at woodworking designs or shopping for timber, you'll find it listed by depth and breadth (for example, 13, 24, 18, and so on). However, if you measure the boards, you'll see that they aren't the same size as the ones described. These boards are referred to as dimensional lumber.

- Softwoods and hardwoods are the two forms of lumber.

Softwoods

Conifer trees such as pine, fir, spruce, and cedar provide softwood timber. These woods are classified as such because they may readily be damaged with your fingernail. A list of common softwood types and their features is provided below:

Western Cedar

Since it can withstand damp settings without decaying, red cedar is often used for outdoor furniture, decks, and building exteriors.

Fir Wood

Fir is most often used for construction, but it's also affordable and may be used to make furniture. Its grain pattern isn't very appealing, and it doesn't absorb stain well; therefore, it's recommended to use it only when the final product is painted.

Pine Wood

Since it's simple to shape and stain, pine is widely used in furniture. Most home centers sell pine, but it's usually lower quality than what you'd buy at a good lumberyard.

Hardwoods

Hardwoods are popular among woodworkers. Colors, textures, and grain patterns come together to create attractive and intriguing furniture. A list of common hardwoods and their qualities follow:

Birch Wood

Birch is a cheap wood, yet it's so beautiful that it's often made of great furniture. Birch is sturdy and easy-to-work-with wood. However, since it is difficult to stain and may become blotchy, you may want to paint anything made of birch.

Mahogany

The wood has a reddish-brown to deep-red color, a straight grain, and a medium texture, making it one of the best furniture woods. The only disadvantage is that mahogany is not cultivated in environmentally-friendly woods.

Oak Wood

Oak is one of the most popular furniture woods. There are two colors to choose from: red and white. Since white oak has a more appealing figure than red oak, it is selected for furniture manufacture. White oak is also moisture resistant and suitable for outdoor furniture. Since many people like the texture of oak, it is widely utilized for flooring and furniture.

ENGINEERED WOODS

Engineered wood, also known as composite wood, manufactured board, or composite wood, is a derivative wood product formed by binding or fastening strands, particles, and other elements together using adhesives or other fixation processes to make composite materials.

Engineered wood products may also be customized to fulfill particular application needs. Even with standard tools, it is simple to work. They are much easier to cut, drill, route, connect, glue, and secure than solid wood.

The most popular engineered woods are

- plywood Blockboard
- board of particles
- fiberboard with a medium density
- fiberboard with a high density
- lumber with laminated veneer

THE FUNDAMENTALS OF JOINERY

A project's joinery may make or break it. In general, the more complex a joint is, the more powerful it is. That's why, throughout the planning phases, woodworkers choose the joints they'll utilize.

Butt Joint: A basic corner or edge-to-edge connection of two pieces of wood. Glue blocks or screws may be used to strengthen it.

Dado Joint: This joint may be found on bookshelf shelves. A dado cut in the other receives the end of one piece.

Lap Joint: You may add bonding surface and strength to a butt joint by cutting a rabbet in the overlapping piece.

The Mortise-and-Tenon Joint: A conventional, sturdy joint that may be strengthened by adding a peg. Mortises do not always go all the way through.

The Tongue-and-Groove Joint: This joint allows for the shrinking of the wood. Cut a track in one piece's edge and a notch to fit into the groove on the other.

WOOD GLUING

Many wood-based tasks need the use of glue. However, finding the finest wood glue for your specific application isn't always straightforward.

- The most prevalent form of wood glue is polyvinyl acetate (PVA). Typical white and yellow glues are included in this category.
- Epoxy is usually divided into two parts: a hardener and a resin. The components are blended to form a chemical bond that is waterproof and fills gaps when it solidifies. Although certain epoxies take a long time to cure, they are among the strongest wood glues available.
- Polyurethane glues are a form of moisture-activated glue that foams up into a strong adhesive when it dries.

CLAMPING WOOD

The Right Angle Clamp makes 90° joint projects quicker and simpler than ever before by helping to keep the components in place while driving in the screws.

Right Angle Clamps: How to Use Them

Step 1: Open the clamp

Turn the handle counterclockwise to open the clamp. Continue to twist the clamp until it is broader than the wood pieces you're attaching.

Step 2: Arrange and glue the wood

Place the wood in a square and attach it with a slight coating of wood glue so the pieces meet at a straight angle. Once your clamps are set, you can quickly wash away any excess wood glue with a moist cloth.

Step 3: Tighten the clamp

Place the clamp on the right and left sides of the right angle, respectively. Tighten the clamp by twisting the handle until the piece is secure. Keep the object fastened for at least two hours after the wood glue has dried.

WOOD STAINING

New wood must first be sanded to get a fantastic, smooth surface. Sanding will assist in leveling out the surface, giving it a wonderful silky finish for the into which the stain will sink. The wood may be painted or varnished if it is old. If this is the case, use a paint and varnish remover to remove any previous coats. Alternatively, if the wood has been treated with an oil or wax, remove it using mineral spirit—sand smooth after removing the previous finish.

Putting the Stain On

Use a foam brush or a lint-free cloth to apply the wood stain (you can also use a regular bristle brush). Allow it to sink into the wood for a few minutes before wiping away any excess with a clean towel. The deeper the color, the longer you let the stain soak in before wiping away any excess. You can achieve a deeper color by applying many layers.

Finishing

For the greatest effects, you should finish the wood after staining it. A wood finish will provide extra wood protection while also enhancing the color of the wood stain.

STARTING EASY

Rack for Magazines

You can build a magazine rack in two or three nights of tinkering in the workshop. It also serves as a way to keep magazines off your living room coffee table or your bedroom nightstand. It's made up of two identical 3-piece frames that are connected by a self-locking half-lap.

How to Fix a Squeaky Bed

Here are a few fast and easy remedies that you probably already have around the home to help you sleep well.

Tighten the Joints

Fixing a noisy bed may sometimes be as easy as tightening a few screws and nuts. Examine all of the joints on your bed frame and pull any that are loose using a tool or screwdriver. To get a tighter fit, consider adding washers to the screws. They function if they are made of plastic or rubber.

Wax

Wax works wonders for noisy mattresses, just as it does for sticky dresser drawers. When you've figured out which joint is making the noise, brush a candlestick or a bar of paraffin or beeswax all over the joint's contact surfaces. You may need to disassemble the joint depending on the sort of bed frame you have. To get rid of the friction generating the sound, you may need to apply numerous applications.

Oil

You can stop the squeaking from metal bed parts by oiling the joints or springs. A few drops of vegetable oil or a WD-40 spray can lubricate the joints and keep them quiet.

Remove Water Stains From Wood

Use a Blow Dryer

Set your hair dryer to the lowest setting possible and aim it towards the water ring. Make careful to shift the dryer around to avoid direct heat and overheating the wood.

Petroleum Jelly or Mayonnaise

Using a soft cloth, dab a dab of each material onto the spot and massage it in a circular motion. If the discoloration persists, add extra product and leave it on for an hour or two, or even overnight.

Restore Dull Furniture Finishes

Step 1: Remove the old finish

Dissolve and remove the previous coatings using a semi-paste stripper to prepare them for scraping. You'll need to remove the old finish first to create a place for the new one. Depending on the thickness of the original finish, you should let it rest anywhere from five minutes to half an hour.

To remove any leftover particles of the finish, use a liquid-form stripper.

Step 2: Apply a fresh coat

Now that the wood has been stripped of its finish, it's time to apply a fresh coat. While penetrating finishes seem more natural, use one of the surface finishes if you want long-lasting protection—even if it isn't nearly as natural-looking:

- Shellac has low water resistance.
- Lacquer is the most common professional finish.
- Polyurethane, particularly oil-based polyurethane, is very durable and user-friendly.

Keep track of how many coatings of polyurethane you apply. You'll need anything from three to six coats of polyurethane, depending on the brand you select—but two is the absolute least.

15

CABINETS & COUNTERS

Storage space is always limited in an apartment. Making your storage cabinets gives you more control over your spending. If you run out of money, you may always put the project on hold for a while and resume it once you have the necessary finances. You may also invest in long-lasting and robust DIY items that will readily pay for themselves.

HOW TO CONSTRUCT A TV STAND

Step 1: Decide on the kind of construction material you want to use

In this scenario, plywood will suffice. When it comes to constructing furniture, plywood is a great option. Plywood is also a good choice for folks who aren't exceptionally proficient at working with tools. When it comes to do-it-yourself projects, plywood is also a lot simpler to work with than hardwood.

Step 2: Mill the components making use of the cut list

Begin by dismantling all of the massive sheets of plywood you have on hand. For this project, a table saw is a solid alternative to consider. Also, attempt to figure out how big your stand will need to be. Consider the size of the TV, shelves, and all other items you'll be storing on the stand.

Step 3: Use a table saw to make sliding doors

Your TV stand will look fantastic with sliding doors. Given the doors glide open and closed quickly, there's no danger of them being wrenched open or banged shut too violently. Mark the grooves where you'll be making cuts to make the sliding doors easier to operate.

Step 4: Plywood joinery with brass rods

Before the cabinets are cemented up, try to finish sanding the interior of the stand. After cutting the brass, glue it with epoxy. Connect the brass to the dividers and joints. After you've cut and put the brass, all you have to do now is sand the whole surface.

Step 5: Put the skeleton and the doors together

Now, the TV stand starts to take form. First, assemble the skeleton of the stand. Imagine how it will appear when it is finished, and then build the mainframe wherever the stand will be. Also, make sure the doors are correctly installed on the front part.

Step 6: Join the back and base together

Join the back and base together using glue and nails. At this point, the overall design begins to take shape. Position the rear of the stand in place and secure it, then go on to the base. Use tiny nails to attach all other frame elements to the bottom after the base is in place for stability.

Step 7: Sand and finish the parts

After you've finished putting everything together, give it a good sanding on both the interior and exterior. Sanding will provide a smooth finish to the stand. After you've sanded it, you may apply your finishing touches, like paints or patterns.

CONSTRUCTION OF A BATHROOM CABINET

To cut the trim, you'll need a miter saw. You can save time by using a table saw and a brad nailer, but you can instead use a circular saw and drive the nails by hand if you prefer.

Depending on the bifold doors available at your home store, the height and breadth of your cabinet may fluctuate somewhat from our specifications. So first pick your doors, then adjust the lengths of the sides, top, bottom, and center shelves as needed. Bifold closet doors are usually supplied in pairs, with hinges connecting them. Each of our doors was

11-15/16 inches wide, and we trimmed them to length as indicated below.

Cabinet door construction is a time-consuming and challenging task. However, you may save time and effort by purchasing closet doors and trimming them to suit the cabinet. It's quick and easy using store-bought closet doors.

Step 1: Create a simple box

To make the plywood sections fit together, cut them to size. If you don't have a table saw, you can use a circular saw to create long, straight cuts.

Step 2: Put the cabinet together

Use glue and screws to assemble the cabinet box, then add wood dowels for further support. Long dowels may be purchased and chopped into small pieces. However, pre-cut and fluted dowels for woodworking are simpler to use. This technique of assembly is fast and simple, and it produces excellent results. However, since the procedure requires a lot of wood filler to cover the fasteners, it's only suitable for painted work.

Using a drill bit that can make both pilots and countersink holes simultaneously, drill 1/8-in. Pilot and countersink holes for the screws. Attach one side's top, bottom, and cleats before adding the other. Mark the location of the center shelf on the sides, then slide it into place and secure it with screws.

Take diagonal measures to ensure the box is square; equal measurements indicate the box is square. To keep the box square, screw a piece of plywood diagonally across the rear of it. Drill the dowel holes using a 3/8-inch. Brad-point bit for clean, splinter-free holes, drilling the holes 1/8 inch deeper than the length of the dowels. You may then sink the dowels below the plywood's surface and fill the holes with wood filler.

Step 3: Make shelf support holes using a drill

Drill holes for the adjustable shelf support with a brad-point drill bit after the box is finished. A 1/4-inch hole is required for most shelf supports. Using a piece of pegboard to place the holes, drill shelf support holes. To avoid piercing all the way through, wrap masking tape around the drill bit.

Step 4: Make the cabinet doors.

To achieve a straight cut, use a handmade saw guide to cut the doors. Screw a straight 1x3 to a 14x18-inch scrap of 3/4-inch plywood to form a guide. Then cut off the extra plywood with your saw along the 1x3 to make a guide that keeps your saw completely straight and specifies the precise direction of the cut. Mark the doors, line up the part with the markings, clamp the guide in place, and cut.

Step 5: Install hinges on the doors

Three inches from the ends, screw the hinges to the doors. For correctly positioned hinges, use a self-centering drill bit to locate the screw holes. Louvered doors have comparable fronts and backs, so double-check before drilling. Place the doors against the cabinet and place spacers between them to create a 1/8-inch gap at the bottom. A 1/8-inch space between the doors is also recommended.

Step 6: Put the doors in the right place

For a failsafe, precise fit, screw the hinges to the cabinet from the inside. Screw the hinges into place after clamping each door into place. Don't worry if the doors don't line up correctly since the box is a little out of square; you can square it up after you hang it. Also, you can adjust the hinges 1/16 inch up or down.

Step 7: Cut the crown molding to size

Cut the plywood crown and base frames to the same size as the cabinet's top. Cut the crown molding upside down and against the fence with your miter saw set to 45 degrees. Clamp a block to the wall to keep the molding securely in place. Miter a tester strip of molding to aid in placing the side pieces when they are nailed in place.

Step 8: Attach the crown molding to the frame using nails

Attach the crown to the frame using a nail. Only use pins to secure the mitered corners if required. Allow the glue to keep them together if they fit snugly and are precisely aligned.

Step 9: Place the crown molding in the middle

You can pre-drill nail holes to reduce splitting while installing crown molding. Install the front piece of crown molding once the sides are in place. Cut it slightly longer and then use your miter saw to "shave" one end till it fits appropriately. The crown should be centered on the cabinet and secured with screws pushed from the inside. The cabinet should then be centered on the foundation and attached in the same manner. Screw both the base and the crown to the cabinet.

Painting louvered doors by hand is time-consuming and inconvenient, but you may save time and effort using spray primer and paint. With 120-grit paper, sand the cabinet box, crown, base, and doors. Apply a white stain-blocking primer to all of the pieces. After the primer has dried, softly sand it with a small sanding sponge. Finally, apply at least two coats of spray paint to the surface.

Locate studs and put two 3-inch screws through the top cleat to hang the cabinet. After that, rehang the doors. Ensure they fit correctly by closing them. You can nudge the bottom left or right of the square, the cabinet, and the doors. Use the bottom cleat to drive screws.

REPAIRING YOUR KITCHEN CABINETS

While most contemporary fitted kitchens are built to survive regular use and abuse, an older kitchen may be seeing some wear and tear. We've compiled a list of fast and simple do-it-yourself fixes that you can do in a single day.

Tighten the Screws

There is a remedy if your cabinet hinges are loose or if the screws in your hinges spin but don't tighten and the screw hole is stripped. Remove the hardware and pack as many toothpicks as fit into the hole with a drop of wood glue on the ends. Remove any extra adhesive with a damp cloth. Allow the adhesive to dry before cutting flush with the cabinet or drawer using a craft knife. Reinstall the hardware by screwing it into the fill hole.

Fill In The Blanks

If your cabinets are dirty and have a lot of scratches, it's time to think about giving them a facelift. Use a furniture repair crayon to repair scratches on kitchen cabinets. They are available in a variety of wood tones to complement your current finish.

Catch That No Longer Keeps a Door Closed

A damaged or out-of-adjusted catch that no longer holds a door closed. Since catches are secured with two screws, repairing a broken one is straightforward. Adjustment is precise, although you may need to re-adjust the catch a few times before getting it exactly right. Tighten the screws after loosening them and moving the catch in or out. Try again if the door does not shut securely.

Broken Drawer

Drawer bottoms are made of a thin board that may get wavy or even fall out. Use thin plywood or MDF to stiffen the bottoms. Cut the board to fit over the bottom of the drawer, leaving a 3mm space on each side. Place the board on the bottom of the drawer and apply wood glue. Once the glue has dried, clamp the board into place.

Even for an experienced carpenter, constructing kitchen cabinets may be a significant task. Cabinetmaking is not difficult since it entails repeatedly building simple box forms. If you're creating kitchen cabinets for the first time, you may want to hire a professional to help you with this challenging task. If you don't have time or basic carpentry abilities, consider utilizing pre-existing cabinet drawers and doors or even remodeling old kitchen cabinets into new ones.

ROOF REPAIRS AND IMPROVEMENTS

Thinking about how to roof a home might make you feel overwhelmed. On the other hand, a simple roof installation may be accomplished if you invest time and finances. Anyone who possesses all of the essential tools, and a strong eye for detail, is competent to install or repair a roof.

WORKING ON YOUR ROOF

Take Safety Measures

Being on a roof puts the body in uncomfortable and dangerous situations. To avoid sliding, use shoes with a rubber sole. Always work with a partner and wear a harness.

Roof-Spraying

Go up to the roof with a garden hose and start spraying in various spots to discover the leak. If it's winter, hold off since it's dangerous to run water on the roof while it's below freezing.

Keep Gutters in Good Shape

Clogged gutters are one of the most typical sites and sources of roof leaks. Water may build up in clogged gutters during a rainstorm.

Avoid Dry Rot

If a roof repair is being performed in the center of the roof, the plywood may be decaying. The roof will droop, causing the roof shingles to become brittle, break, and leak. The rot is caused by insufficient air rather than any form of water damage. Installing a ridge vent, which will only operate with a soffit vent, is the best way to prevent dry rot.

Check Leaks In Valleys

A valley is defined as the point where two roofs meet. It's also known as the ridge since it's where two roofs meet at the top. Valleys are particular sites for leaks since that's where all of the roof's water flows and starts sloshing back and forth.

REPAIRING GUTTERS

Gutter cleaning isn't the most glamorous chore, but it's necessary for general home care, and, fortunately, it doesn't have to be tough. Here's a step-by-step approach to cleaning your roof gutters:

1. Place your ladder securely against the gutter section you wish to clean. Make sure it's secured with a ladder strap and that someone is holding it at the bottom.
2. With your gloves on and a garbage bag or container, climb the ladder.
3. Scoop out the trash with your hands or a tiny shovel.
4. Fill your bucket or trash bag with the contents of your scoop.
5. Climb down, relocate the ladder to a different spot, and start cleaning again once that area is clear.
6. Do cleaning short bursts since reaching too far up a ladder might easily result in a fall.

CLEANING A ROOF

1. Once the gutters are empty, rinse them out to eliminate any remaining debris and check for leaks.
2. Check the downpipes for any clogs and clear them out with pressurized water or your hands.
3. Consider removing moss from roof tiles for a

complete roof and gutter cleaning. Removing moss will enhance the appearance of your home while also preventing it from falling into the gutters and clogging them.

HOW TO INSTALL GUTTERS ON YOUR HOME

Step 1: Make a drawing and take measurements of your home

Make a note of the length of the gutter runs and the positions of the downspouts. Measure the height of the downspouts. Add the extension away from the house at the bottom by 16 to 20 inches each. After that, add up the inner and outside corners, as well as the end caps. Downspouts should be placed in places where water will run away from home. Avoid areas where there are barriers and especially avoid electric meters.

Step 2: Pre-assemble your gutters

Working from the ground is considerably easier than working from the top of a ladder. As the manufacturer recommends, instead of putting components together and concealing the joints with a seam cover, overlap all seams by a foot and then rivet and seal them together. To prevent water from being driven out the seam, overlap the gutters such that the inner part faces downhill.

Step 3: Cut in downspout tubes

Measure from the corner of your home to the center of the downspout site. Make sure there aren't any impediments. Cut a downspout outlet into the gutter using this measurement.

Step 4: Install a trim or fascia board

A trim or fascia board is usually installed directly under the roof tiles on many residences. You'll need to inspect it and replace it if required, or you'll need to install one if you don't already have one. Before hanging gutters, prime and paint bare wood or cement fiberboard.

Hang the downspouts to complete the gutter work. The downspouts should be attached to the wall. If you can't locate U-shaped brackets, you may create your own out of downspout pieces. They're more appealing than the outside-wrapping bands.

Take your time and effort while installing gutters to ensure that they are installed correctly. During a hard rainfall, a drain that is not firmly secured may come off. The gutter might potentially become loose due to wind or other weather conditions. A loose gutter might lead to water accumulation and puddles. Heavy rain will not destroy a gutter that is firmly fastened.

REPAIRING DAMAGED ROOF SHINGLES

STEP 1

Make sure the nails are firmly lodged in the felt and sheathing while installing shingles. The sun's heat causes shingles to expand with time, causing the nails to pop out of position and increasing the danger of a leak. Since the roof is slanted, make sure the shingles are layered from bottom to top, with the top set overhanging the bottom. You may rent a roofing nail gun.

STEP 2

Lay down a foundation after removing the debris and re-framing the roof (sheathing). The sheathing is typically made of eight-foot-long, 1/2-inch-thick plywood. Measure the aperture of the shingled roof portion, cut the plywood to size, then attach the plywood to the roof rafters. For added strength, stagger the sheathing in a brick pattern. Avoid putting a full 8-foot length of plywood on the roof. The midsection of such a lengthy composition is structurally unsound. Continue to place the plywood seams in a brick pattern until the open space is covered.

STEP 3

Begin by stapling the 6-inch starting strip to the lowest portion of the roof, allowing a 1-inch overhang on the eave to ensure gutter drainage. Lay and nail the remaining felt layers with a 2-inch overlap from the bottom up. To guarantee optimum retention, nail the tar strip to each felt layer.

STEP 4

Begin laying the first row of shingles at the roof's bottom corner. Start with a base row of shingles and work your way up in a pyramid form, following the chalk lines. To achieve optimal grip, use six nails per shingle and always nail on the tar strip. Following your first pyramid foundation, continue working your way across and up the roof. If you're replacing shingles on an area of your roof that's been damaged, make sure you put the old ones on top of the new ones. This placement will give a consistent and smooth appearance.

KEEPING ICE DAMS FROM FORMING

Reduce Snow Load

Snow on your roof should be kept to a minimum to avoid ice dams. Clear snow from your roof using a roof rake or call a specialist.

Keep Your Attic Ventilated

Insulate and ventilate your attic. Without it, your home's heat will flow into the attic, melting the snow on the roof. We suggest a roofing contractor check the airflow.

How to Boost Attic Airflow

Installing Roof Vent Fans

In addition to spherical forms, there are square variants with a lower profile that are less visually invasive. These are put as near to the ridgeline as feasible. They work well at expelling heated air, although others find them unappealing.

Installing a roof vent fan

1. Mark The midpoint of each roof vent by a nail driven into the roof from inside the attic. Put a nail up through the roof from the inside next to each rafter. Now you know where the rafters are and where your roof vent will be.
2. Cut through the shingles using a utility knife after marking the vent opening on the roof.
3. Cut the plywood with a jigsaw.
4. Apply Roof cement to the underside of the horizontal flange of the vent. Next, slide the top of the flange under the shingles above the opening.
5. Add a bead of roof cement along the edge of the vent and the shingles to secure the vent to the roof.

HOW TO INSTALL A SKYLIGHT

Installing a skylight is not a simple undertaking since it entails cutting the roof, building new structural framework members, installing drywall, and completing the ceiling underneath the skylight. You must properly fit the metal flashing and roofing paper; otherwise, the roof may leak around the skylight. If you have strong carpentry abilities, follow the manufacturer's guidelines carefully; otherwise, employ a professional.

Step 1: Cut and frame the opening

Follow the manufacturer's guidelines for cutting the hole in your roof. Use a circular saw to cut the aperture in the roof from the inside, then drill a locating hole in the roof where you want the center of the skylight to be. Frame the area, so it is structurally sound according to building requirements. Be cautious about supporting the ends of roof rafters before cutting and removing them! Install header joists perpendicular to the remainder of the beams.

If the skylight is situated above an attic, you'll also have to cut and frame a hole in the ceiling of the area below it and build a light shaft through the attic. Contact a professional constructor if you're not acquainted with fundamental carpentry methods or building a huge skylight that will require you to remove more than one rafter.

Step 2: Cut back the roofing and connect the skylight

To cut roof shingles, use a utility knife and a straightedge to cut approximately 3 inches back from the aperture on all four sides. Set the skylight in position, centered on the aperture, and secure it to the roof using nails or screws.

Step 3: Slip in the underlayment

Under the shingles, slide 8-inch broad pieces of roofing paper. Install the bottom, then the sides, and finally the top. The objective is to overlap the down-roof with the up-roof to shed water adequately. Achieving this will require some skill. Lift any obstructions with a flat pry bar, taking care not to harm the shingles.

Step 4: Step flashing

Glue a single piece of bottom flashing to the roof shingles, partially surrounding the skylight. Don't glue vertically through the roof but horizontally into the skylight. Next, slide step flashing beneath the shingles. Each side works up from the bottom. The step flashing sections must be four inches apart.

Step 5: Set up the solid flashing

Do so by sliding it under the roof and connecting it to the skylight. First the bottom, then the sides. Water cannot penetrate between the step flashing and the skylight because of these parts.

CLEANING YOUR CHIMNEY

Chimney cleaning isn't as simple as it seems, and expertise matters. Buy a chimney brush that fits your chimney and extra extension rods for cleaning the whole chimney. Use a metal brush for masonry and a poly brush for stainless steel flues.

How to use a chimney brush

1. Close the fireplace door or tape plastic over the aperture.
2. The first rod threaded from above, with the damper open and the chimney cap removed.
3. Insert the brush into the flue and scrape up and down.
4. Add more rods if required and keep scrubbing until you reach the bottom.
5. Once the brush is out, inspect the chimney for creosote. If not, repeat the steps.
6. After cleaning the chimney, use a shop vacuum to remove any soot and creosote from the lower sections.

MAINTAINING YOUR ROOF AND GUTTERS

You need to maintain your roof and gutters after cleaning them. Follow these tips

- Your gutters should be cleaned twice a year at the very least.
- Try pouring food-colored water down your gutters to find leaks. You'll be able to see where the holes are much more easily.

- It would be best if you trimmed trees that hang directly over your roof to prevent leaf debris from falling on your house.

Performing regular maintenance on a roof can be time-consuming. But failing to do it can become very expensive. Keep in mind that you will benefit from preventative work, not just this year but also for many years to come.

17

EXTERIORS AND BACKYARD

It's time to take advantage of the better weather by working on a few exterior house renovations.

REPLACING VINYL SIDING

While vinyl may be a terrific alternative to regular home paint, it does come with a cost. Although it seems to be traditional siding from a distance, the illusion is broken at corners, windows, doors, and utility equipment installed on the wall.

Since the siding must be laid on a level surface, you'll need to line the walls with rigid foam board, generally, 1/2-inch thick unless you're siding a new house or have removed the previous lap siding. While rigid foam provides some insulation, it is mainly used to provide a level nailing surface. Use galvanized shingle nails to secure the stiff foam and siding. Continue by following these steps:

1. Vinyl siding is nailed via a nailing strip when it is installed initially. The nailing strip of the course below is secured onto the bottom of the following course.
2. When replacing siding, choose a piece made by the same company and has the same color.
3. Release the siding from the nailing strip after working your hand into a seam between sections.
4. Remove the damaged siding by pulling the nails holding it in place.
5. Insert the new piece into the course's nailing strip.
6. Allow for expansion and contraction by lightly nailing the siding.
7. If the whole piece of siding isn't destroyed, a utility knife and speed square may cut away the damaged area.
8. Make the patch as long as possible. To allow for expansion and contraction, remove a portion of the nailing strip from the rear.
9. Use a zip tool to secure the last component in place.

PATCHING WOOD SIDING

Any substance meant for outdoor usage will break and wash away quickly. Outside fillers should be waterproof and flexible. Stucco and caulk for the outside suit the criteria, but they never solidify and are impossible to form. An epoxy filler that cures solid hardness is the ideal filler for your siding.

Remove Loose Paint

With a putty knife or paint scraper, remove any loose paint from the repair area.

Remove Rot with a Screwdriver

When you need to repair a hole in wood siding, use an awl or a flat-head screwdriver to dig out all the rot from within the crack or hole. It's critical to remove all decay; otherwise, it will continue to develop under the filler.

The Siding Should Be Sanded

Remove splinters and produce a smooth surface for the filler with 120-grit sandpaper.

Fill in the Blanks

Mix epoxy wood filler and hardener in the quantities suggested on the package. Prepare only as much external wood filler as you'll need since you'll have to throw away whatever you don't use.

To apply the filler, put on a pair of rubber gloves. Some products resemble putty and may be rolled into a ball and stuffed into the hole with your fingers, while others are more pastelike and need the use of a putty knife to apply.

Fill Gaps With Exterior Wood Filler

Using a putty knife or a tiny disposable brush, rough shape the putty to fit the surrounding siding shapes. If you're using a pastelike product, you'll probably need to wait five minutes for it to harden.

Allow For the Hardening of the Filler

Allow the filler to set, which may take 20 minutes to four hours, depending on the product. Fine-tune the form with a rasp or file, then sand the filler and surrounding siding using 120-grit sandpaper. Complete the project by repainting the area to match the color of the external siding.

REPAIRING STUCCO

Step 1: Remove loosened stucco

Using a hammer or a cold chisel, knock off the loose stucco. Be careful not to harm the underlying wood lath supports. It is necessary to use eye protection.

Step 2: Remove the edges by chipping away at them

Continue until the stucco is securely attached to the lath. Use tin Snips to cut any protruding metal mesh.

Step 3: Cover the lath that has been exposed

Trim a piece of grade-D builder's paper to fit closely at the border where the old stucco meets the exposed wood lath using a utility knife. Roofing nails should be used to secure the paper to the lath, and then place the second layer of paper on top of the first.

Step 4: Install Mesh

Place galvanized metal lath over the paper and trim it close to the stucco's border. Drive more roofing nails through the mesh and into the wood lath. This work will be made simpler using snips with offset handles.

Step 5: Combine the stucco ingredients

Make a batch of stucco according to the first-coat formula, using a wheelbarrow as a mixing bowl. The acrylic bonding agent used in this mixture increases the new stucco's adherence to the existing plaster.

Step 6: Sling it

Wet the old stucco's edge to prevent it from sucking moisture out of the patch and weakening the link between the old and new. Using a brick trowel, scoop fist-size wads of wet stucco and hurl them against the wire lath until it's fully coated. Smooth the mixture with a finishing trowel, then use a brick trowel to pack it against the previous stucco's edge. Continue to add material until the layer is approximately 1/2 inch below the previous stucco.

Step 7: Scratch it

Score the patch's surface after it loses its wet shine to strengthen the connection to the next application. Use plastic wrap to protect it from drying out.

Step 8: Apply a second coat of paint

Remove the plastic after seven days and spray the spot with water. Make a batch of stucco according to the second-coat formula. Trowel on a 3/8-inch-thick layer, starting at the bottom and working your way up. With a brick trowel, smooth down the edges. Wait for the wet sheen to go away before troweling the spot smooth, slightly below the current stucco level. Cover with a plastic sheet once more.

Step 9: Apply the sealing coat

Remove the plastic after three days, spray the spot, and make a new batch of stucco according to the finish-coat formula. Various textures need different approaches. Scoop little globs of wet mix onto his brick trowel and flicked them against the wall until they were level with the previous surface to resemble the wall's original "dash" finish.

Allow a week for the repair to dry before painting it and the remainder of the wall. The patch is almost unnoticeable under a layer of heavy-bodied acrylic elastomer.

TRIM AN EXTERIOR WINDOW

If you want to install vinyl window trim to your house with vinyl siding, you must first remove the old siding and J-channel from around the windows. Be cautious when removing the siding since you'll need to replace it once the new trim is done. Then, while leaving the windowsill in place, remove the metal flashing that covers it and nail your new vinyl windowsill on top. Glue vinyl end caps to either end of your new windowsill after it's secure.

Install the casing around the window's sides and top next. Begin with the vertical sides, adjusting the length and design of the bottom before anchoring it to your house. After you've completed both sides of the window, go on to the top.

You're now ready to start working on your new molding. Beginning with the two vertical sides, be sure you measure and cut your molding to the proper size. Cut the horizontal piece to fit over the vertical moldings and snap it in place. Place the final piece of molding on top of the window and note where the vertical moldings will meet it once they are in place.

To prevent water from seeping into your house, cut and install new J-channels before replacing the siding. The last step is to replace the siding you took off. You may have to reduce this to fit around your new trim.

BUILDING DECK STAIRS

Carpenters are assessed based on their completed projects, the items in their toolboxes, and their ability to construct stairs. Building porch stairs, regardless of ability level, is still within reach of the ordinary do-it-yourselfer.

It is important to become familiar with the components of a series of steps:

- The rise refers to the height of the porch or stairs you'll require.
- The length of the stairs from the porch's edge to the ground is known as a run.
- The tread and riser are commonly joined to stringers, which are 2 x 12-inch treated wood planks. Pre-cut stringers are available at most lumber and home improvement shops.
- The treads are made up of 2 x 6-inch treated wood planks laid parallel to make a single 10.5-inch broad step.
- A riser, which looks like a toe board, will be attached to the rear or upright part of the step. The majority of the stairs are 6 to 8 inches tall.

Porch Steps Construction

1. Calculate the distance between the steps (how long

they will be). Also, check your local ordinances for details on railing requirements and permits.
2. Using a 4-foot level, put the level on the top of the porch and measure the distance to the ground.
3. Divide the overall height by the riser height to get the riser height. The answer will inform you how many steps you'll need.
4. Keep in mind that the riser height ranges from 6 to 8 inches. Let's use 35 inches as an example height from the porch to the ground. Thirty-five inches divided by the riser height of 7 inches will require five equal steps.
5. Remember to consider the apron or block at the foot of the steps to help support the stairs.
6. Multiply five steps by 10.5 inches to give you the run. The run in our example is 52.5 inches.
7. Using a carpenter's square, lay out the steps to be cut from the stringer.
8. Clamp a straight edge at the 7-inch point on the short outer part of the square to set it up.
9. At that time, the square's extended outer portion will be at 10.5 inches.
10. Place the square along the stringer's edge and begin marking the five steps from the end.
11. Cut out the steps with a circular saw and square up the stringer ends to the stairs.
12. Make a pattern out of the first stringer you cut out. For maximum strength, space stringers no more

than 16 inches apart. A 4-foot-wide stair would need four stringers.
13. Stringers are attached to the porch with metal hangers and 1.5-inch deck screws.
14. As you continue, double-check that they're plumb and level with each other.
15. The bottoms of the stringers should not be lying on the ground but rather on a concrete pad or brick foundation.
16. Use 2.5-inch deck screws to connect the riser board (cut to the length and breadth required).
17. Install the two×6-inch treads parallel to each other, with 1/8 inch between the boards.
18. Use 2.5-inch deck screws to secure the treads to the stringers.
19. Apply a weatherproof deck stain or porch paint to the surface.

CONSTRUCT A NATURAL GARDEN WALKWAY

A stone walkway has a rustic look that works well in a cottage garden design or natural landscape design. A simple handset pathway is a great do-it-yourself project.

Prepare the Path

Mark your path with pegs and string or two garden hoses. If the path is often used between a driveway and a front door, make sure it is wide enough for two people to cross comfortably. A lone traveler may take little garden paths or roads to hidden natural corners. Make sure both sides have hoses or strings.

Excavate a Road for Yourself

Follow the ropes or garden hoses to cut through the grass around the path's edges. Remove all grass and vegetation, including roots, off the path. Dig a five-inch deep level, smooth foundation (for three-inch-thick stone). Tamp the dirt using a hand tamp or by stepping over it.

Use Landscape Fabric

Cover the path with landscaping cloth. Whenever feasible, use a continuous piece. For many parts, space the edges at least 12 inches apart. Trim the fabric along the path's sides with a utility knife and staple it to the earth.

Sand the Surface

Smooth the sand using a 2x4 board somewhat smaller than the route's width.

Set the Stones

Place the route stones along one side of the walkway. The goal is to see each stone's size and shape before building the route so you can choose the best fit.

Begin putting stones in the sand bed of the path. If you wish to fill in the gaps with sand or gravel, leave tiny gaps between the rocks. Place each rock so that it is level and stable. Use a carpenter's level to verify each stone's level and level nearby rocks.

Spread the sand with a brush, wet the route to settle it, and fill in the sand gaps. If desired, fill up the gaps with sand or gravel. Add a potting soil mix beside the walkway before putting plants like sedum or bugleweed.

CONCLUSION

DIY renovations are a terrific way to save money, feel accomplished, and include the whole family, but they may be devastating if you don't know what you're doing. Determine which activities you can safely do and which should be left to the professionals, such as a possibly load-bearing wall, asbestos, or lead paint. If you're uncertain, get a skilled contractor to assist you.

While practice can help you complete numerous home repair and remodeling work around your house, certain things are best left to professionals—both for your (and your family's) safety and to ensure an exquisite finish.

THINK OUTSIDE THE BOX

DIY Home renovation entails more than just employing equipment and abilities to make things happen; it also entails understanding the issue and devising innovative solutions. Many people believe that renovation projects must be expensive to be effective, but this is not always the case.

Cabinets in the kitchen are a good example: Color and pattern are effective methods to add visual appeal to a space while removing outmoded finishes. Inside these cabinets, a calm geometric wallpaper complements the vibrant turquoise fronts and sides for a joyful visual boost. The appeal of DIY is that you may experiment with materials and equipment to do tasks uniquely and creatively. As you go through each job, you'll see that there are a variety of creative alternatives to do things differently.

INCREASING THE VALUE OF YOUR HOME

Regular house maintenance is the most fundamental and crucial step in ensuring your home's value is preserved.

Maintaining your gutters and drains is essential to keeping them in excellent working order. Replacing old roof tiles and ensuring that walls and fences are in good shape will keep your property safe in bad weather and ensure that it looks attractive to prospective buyers if you decide to sell.

Another option to raise the value of your property is to renovate or build on it. Adding a garden apartment or home office, expanding your house to add a bedroom or bathroom, or just updating your kitchen are all good methods to boost the value of your home. Doing thorough research is necessary since home renovation done incorrectly will lose you money rather than creating value.

If you consider selling your home or want to make some improvements, it's crucial to understand how the modifications will affect its value.

- Before you start tearing down walls, have a professional architect check over your ideas.
- If you want help, always engage competent, respected contractors.
- Have your construction designs authorized by your state to ensure that they are lawful.
- Make sure you have adequate funds on hand to complete your job.

I hope that this book has helped you discover a new enthusiasm for improving different elements of your house and that home remodeling can be a very reasonable and economic undertaking. I'd love to hear about your experiments, renovations, and improvements to your house. Tell your DIY home remodeling tale on Amazon.com, including what you liked most and any new tricks you found along the road.

Would you please take a second to give this book an honest star rating because ratings are the lifeblood of publishers?

REFERENCES

All Images from https://pixabay.com/ or https://www.istockphoto.com

Banta, J. (2002, April 3). How to Tile a Floor. This Old House. https://www.thisoldhouse.com/flooring/21016706/how-to-tile-a-floor

Baylor, C. (2010, April 22). Types of Wood Species for Woodworking. The Spruce Crafts; TheSpruceCrafts. https://www.thesprucecrafts.com/woodworking-with-various-wood-species-3536919

Baylor, C. (2019). 10 Safety Rules Every Woodworker Should Know. The Spruce Crafts. https://www.thesprucecrafts.com/safety-rules-every-woodworker-should-know-3536833

Bennett, J. (2021, September 10). How to Clean Hardwood Floors for Scuff-Free Shine. Better Homes & Gardens. https://www.bhg.com/homekeeping/house-cleaning/surface/how-to-clean-hardwood-floors/

Better Homes & Garden. (2018, June 18). How to Replace Glass in a Metal Storm Window. Better Homes & Gardens. https://www.bhg.com/home-improvement/windows/window-repair/how-to-replace-glass-in-a-metal-storm-window/

Better Homes & Gardens. (2017, October 23). Everything You Need to Know About Window Materials. Better Homes & Gardens; Better Homes & Gardens. https://www.bhg.com/home-improvement/windows/window-buying-guide/selecting-window-materials/

Bobvila. (2013, July 9). Nail Guide. Bob Vila. https://www.bobvila.com/articles/1206-nail-guide/

Boley, M. (2020, September 24). How to Prevent Water Damage in the House. Family Handyman. https://www.familyhandyman.com/list/prevent-water-damage-while-you-are-away/

Boley, M. (2021, September 18). 19 Handy Hints for DIY Electrical Work. Family Handyman. https://www.familyhandyman.com/list/tips-for-diy-electrical-work/

Brock Builders. (2018, August 17). Securing Your House During Your Home Renovation Project. Northeast Security

Solutions. https://northeastsecuritysolutions.com/5-security-ideas-for-your-home-renovation-project/

Company, B. S. (2021). Why You Must Upgrade Smoke Detectors When You Remodel. Www.brothersservices.com. https://www.brothersservices.com/blog/upgrade-smoke-detectors-when-you-remodel

Cox, D. (n.d.). How to Repair Water Damaged Plaster - Do-it-yourself-help.com. Www.do-It-Yourself-Help.com. Retrieved October 31, 2021, from https://www.do-it-yourself-help.com/how-to-repair-plaster-water-damage.html

Cruz, J. (2021). How to Paint Concrete Floors. Family Handyman. https://www.familyhandyman.com/project/how-to-paint-concrete-floors/

Curtis, W. (2006, April 12). How to Fix Popped Drywall Nails. HowStuffWorks. https://home.howstuffworks.com/home-improvement/home-diy/projects/how-to-fix-popped-nails.htm

David. (2021). 7 Ways to Dramatically Improve Your Front Door Security. Drill Warrior. https://drillwarrior.com/7-ways-to-dramatically-improve-your-front-door-security/

Décor Aid. (2018, October 10). Roof Types | 24 Best Roof Styles + Materials For Your Home. Décor Aid. https://www.decoraid.com/blog/roof-types/

Deeds. (2020, November 6). DIY Renovations? Everything You Wanted to Know (or Not) About Permits. Deeds.com. https://www.deeds.com/articles/diy-renovations-everything-you-wanted-to-know-or-not-about-permits/

DIY Network. (n.d.). Repairing a Kitchen Faucet. DIY. Retrieved October 30, 2021, from https://www.diynetwork.com/how-to/skills-and-know-how/plumbing/repairing-a-kitchen-faucet

DIY Network. (n.d.). How to Install a New Window. DIY. https://www.diynetwork.com/how-to/rooms-and-spaces/doors-and-windows/how-to-install-a-new-window

Engel, A. (2020, April 2). How To Install Door Trim. This Old House. https://www.thisoldhouse.com/doors/21193688/installing-trim-around-a-door

Family Handyman. (n.d.-a). Screen Repair: How to Fix a Window Screen. Family Handyman. Retrieved October 29, 2021, from https://www.familyhandyman.com/project/how-to-fix-a-window-screen/

Family Handyman. (n.d.-b). Structural Screws vs. Lag Screws. Family Handyman. Retrieved October 28, 2021, from https://www.familyhandyman.com/project/structural-screws-vs-lag-screws/

Family Handyman. (2017). How to Trim a Door. In YouTube. https://www.youtube.com/watch?v=_ZoKDvHEiUY

Family Handyman. (2021a). How to Adjust a Mechanical Thermostat. Family Handyman. https://www.familyhandyman.com/project/how-to-adjust-a-mechanical-thermostat/

Family Handyman. (2021b). How to Fix a Running Toilet. Family Handyman. https://www.familyhandyman.com/project/how-to-fix-a-running-toilet/

Family Handyman. (2021c). How to Fix Overflowing Gutters. Family Handyman. https://www.familyhandyman.com/project/gutters-how-to-fix-overflowing-gutters/

Family Handyman. (2021d). How to Refinish Hardwood Floors. Family Handyman. https://www.familyhandyman.com/project/how-to-refinish-hardwood-floors/

Family Handyman. (2021e). Troubleshooting Dead Outlets and What to Do When GFCI Won't Reset. Family Handyman. https://www.familyhandyman.com/project/troubleshooting-dead-outlets/

Family Handyman. (2021f, October 21). 10 Most Common Electrical Mistakes DIYers Make. Family Handyman. https://www.familyhandyman.com/list/top-10-electrical-mistakes/

Formisano, B. (21 C.E., June 21). How to Choose the Right Caulk for Your Next Project. The Spruce. https://www.thespruce.com/select-the-right-caulk-for-the-job-1824846

Formisano, B. (2007, September 6). 8 Tips for Using a Hammer Correctly. The Spruce; The Spruce. https://www.thespruce.com/tips-for-properly-using-a-hammer-1825125

Formisano, B. (2021). How to Replace a Humidifier Evaporator Pad. The Spruce. https://www.thespruce.com/replace-a-humidifier-evaporator-pad-1824747

Gillies, M. (2019, November 29). 20 Tips for Planning a Successful House Remodel. Family Handyman. https://www.familyhandyman.com/list/20-tips-for-planning-a-successful-house-remodel/

Glass, D. (2018, April 13). Glass Cleaning & Maintenance Tips. Www.dillmeierglass.com. https://www.dillmeierglass.com/news/glass-cleaning-maintenance-tips

Handyman Connections. (2016, August 23). 7 Safety Tips for Home Repairs. Handyman Connection of Santa Clarita Valley. https://handymanconnection.com/santa-clarita/2016/08/7-safety-tips-for-home-repairs/

Happy Hiller. (2017, June 1). 5 Natural Ways to Unclog a Bathroom Sink | Hiller How-To. Happy Hiller. https://happyhiller.com/blog/5-natural-ways-unclog-bathroom-sink/

Henkenius, M. (2002, March 18). Wallpaper Repairs Made Easy. This Old House. https://www.thisoldhouse.com/walls/21015137/wallpaper-repairs-made-easy

Henkenius, M. (2017, September 25). Improving Attic Ventilation. This Old House. https://www.thisoldhouse.com/heating-cooling/21017397/improving-attic-ventilation

Hill, K. (2018, August 28). How To: Turn Off Your Home's Water. Bob Vila. https://www.bobvila.com/articles/turn-off-water/

Hillcrest Plumbing. (2016, October 15). 18 Beginning Plumbing Tips That Everyone Should Know. Hillcrestplumbing.com. https://hillcrestplumbing.com/beginner-plumbing-tips-that-everyone-should-know/

Holdefehr, K. (2021, September 9). How to Paint a Ceiling—the Easy Way. Real Simple. https://www.realsimple.com/home-organizing/home-improvement/painting/how-to-paint-a-ceiling

Holden, B. (n.d.). How to Fix a Cracked Window. Family Handyman. Retrieved October 29, 2021, from https://www.familyhandyman.com/project/how-to-fix-a-cracked-window/

Home Stratosphere. (2021). 36 Types of Screws and Screw Heads (Ultimate Chart & Guide) - Home Stratosphere. Www.homestratosphere.com. https://www.homestratosphere.com/types-of-screws/

House, T. O. (2002, April 10). A Silent Stair. This Old House. https://www.thisoldhouse.com/stairs/21015214/how-to-fix-squeaky-stairs

House, T. O. (2011, February 4). How to Patch a Sheet Vinyl Floor. This Old House. https://www.thisoldhouse.com/flooring/21017013/how-to-patch-a-sheet-vinyl-floor

How Stuff Works. (2006, May 2). Plumbing Basics. HowStuffWorks. https://home.howstuffworks.com/home-improvement/plumbing/plumbing-basics-ga.htm

How Stuff Works. (2007, March 21). Nails. HowStuffWorks. https://home.howstuffworks.com/nails.htm

Improvenet. (2016, August 10). DIY Safety Tips. Improve-Net. https://www.improvenet.com/a/diy-safety-tips

Johnson, G. (2021). Tips and Techniques for Using a Hammer. VisionAware. https://visionaware.org/everyday-living/home-repairs/gils-guide-to-woodworking/using-a-hammer/

Loushin, S. (2019, April 5). Structural adhesives: A viable alternative to mechanical fasteners. Www.thefabricator.com. https://www.thefabricator.com/thefabricator/article/shopmanagement/structural-adhesives-a-viable-alternative-to-mechanical-fasteners

Madden, G. (2020, December 3). 15 DIY home renovation safety tips. Homes to Love. https://www.homestolove.com.au/home-renovation-safety-19458

Maria. (2018, January 21). Interior Inspiration Archives. The Interior Editor. http://theinterioreditor.com/interior-inspiration/

Maxwell, R. (2021). How to Replace a Doorknob. Family Handyman. https://www.familyhandyman.com/project/how-to-replace-a-doorknob/

Mr Roof. (2021, June 29). Anatomy of a Window. Mr Roof. https://www.mrroof.com/blog/anatomy-of-a-window/

Parker, T. (2021, June 29). Home Improvements That Require Permits. Investopedia. https://www.investopedia.com/financial-edge/1012/home-improvements-that-require-permits.aspx

Plumbing, W. (2021, June 14). How to Install a Whole-House Humidifier. Williams Plumbing. https://www.willplumb.com/how-to-install-a-whole-house-humidifier/

Quigley, A. (2019, January 31). 10 Things Nobody Tells You About Renovating Your Bathroom. Remodelista. https://www.remodelista.com/posts/what-to-know-bathroom-remodel-tips-cost/

Reed, D. (2021). How to Install an Aprilaire Whole-House Humidifier and More. Dengarden. https://dengarden.com/home-improvement/Humidifier-Installing-An-AprilAire-Whole-House-Humidifier

Sonia. (2012, August 3). Glues and Adhesives for Home Improvement. Extreme How To. https://extremehowto.com/glues-adhesives-home-improvement/

Staff, E. I. (2017, July 19). 10 Tips to Renovate your House Beautifully yet Economically. Entrepreneur. https://www.entrepreneur.com/article/297458

Stewart, G. (2020, May 28). 7 Things You MUST Know Before Starting Your Home Renovation. Better Homes & Gardens. https://www.bhg.com/home-improvement/advice/planning/read-this-before-you-start-your-home-renovation-281474979547593/

Stezik, J. (2020, July 9). 6 Ways to Prepare Meals during a Kitchen Renovation. Multi Trade Building Services. https://www.multitradebuildingservices.com/news/ix7sktcvz55h99n1pjmppr7a2ykus4

Stickley, A. (21 C.E., August 9). Here Are 5 Easy Ways to Fix a Leaky PVC Pipe. The Spruce. https://www.thespruce.com/pvc-joint-repair-2718924

Stout, D. (2021, July 7). Buyer's Guide To Flooring Options. Family Handyman. https://www.familyhandyman.com/list/flooring-guide/

Thiele, T. (2019). Learn the Basics of Your Home's Electrical System. The Spruce. https://www.thespruce.com/electrical-basics-101-1152377

Tollsen. (2021, October 6). How to Fix a Squeaky Bed in 5 Steps - Amerisleep. Amerisleep.com. https://amerisleep.com/blog/how-to-fix-a-squeaky-bed/

Truini, J. (2003, April 9). How to Install Rain Gutters. This Old House. https://www.thisoldhouse.com/gutters/21016457/how-to-install-rain-gutters

Truini, J. (2004, August 30). How to Install a Bathroom Vent Fan. This Old House. https://www.thisoldhouse.com/bathrooms/21016701/how-to-install-a-bathroom-vent-fan

Ullman, M. (2020, February 21). 5 Things to Know About Replacing a Garbage Disposal. Bob Vila. https://www.bobvila.com/articles/replacing-a-garbage-disposal/

Vally, N. (2014, August 8). Fix-It Friday: How To Replace A Water Shutoff Valve. Women You Should Know®. https://womenyoushouldknow.net/fix-friday-replace-water-shut-off-valve/

Vandervort, D. (2012, May 27). How to Install a New Dishwasher (or Replace an Old One). HomeTips. https://www.hometips.com/diy-how-to/dishwasher-installing.html

Vandervort, D. (2019). Home Plumbing Systems. HomeTips. https://www.hometips.com/plumbing_fixtures.html

Vandervort, D. (2020, November 25). Interior Doors Buying Guide. HomeTips. https://www.hometips.com/buying-guides/doors-interior.html

Villa, B. (2017, August 15). Solved! What Cracks in the Ceiling Really Mean. Bob Vila. https://www.bobvila.com/articles/cracks-in-ceiling/

Walter, A. (2020, July 3). How to Replace or Repair a Window Pane [Simple DIY Guide]. FAB Glass and Mirror. https://www.fabglassandmirror.com/blog/replacing-and-repairing-window-panes/

Weinberger, D. (2020, December 2). 9 Bathroom Plumbing Mistakes to Avoid. Family Handyman. https://www.familyhandyman.com/article/bathroom-plumbing-mistakes-to-avoid/

Winston Churchill Quotes. (n.d.). BrainyQuote.com. Retrieved November 19, 2021, from BrainyQuote.com Web site: https://www.brainyquote.com/quotes/winston_churchill_143691

Bob has a gift for you - his safety tips. Read the QR code or go to https://bob-hopkins.com/request-bobs-safety-tips.

Printed in Great Britain
by Amazon